GARDEN NOTES
— from —
MUDDY CREEK

A Twelve-Month Guide to
Tending Ornamental Perennnials

Debbie Mahoney Allen
Illustrated by Hannah Firmin

Debbie Allan

FULLER MOUNTAIN PRESS
FERRISBURG, VERMONT

First editor: Terry Allen
Editor: Sharon Faelten
Content Editor: Miranda Fisk
Illustrations: Hannah Firmin

First Edition

Library of Congress Cataloging-in-Publication: 2005939134

First printing, April 2006

Printed in China by Everbest Printing Company Ltd.

ISBN 0-9776372-0-4

Fuller Mountain Press
256 Fuller Mountain Rd.
Ferrisburgh, Vermont 05456

To Terry,

my best friend and true love,
whose generous and loyal nature and boundless
enthusiasm for life endear him to all who know him.

and

Floery, Heather, Heidi and Shannon,

my four ebullient daughters
whose loving hearts, indomitable spirits,
and creative talents never cease to fill me with awe.

Contents

— CONTENTS —

Acknowledgements

My deepest gratitude in creating this book goes to my world-class illustrator, Hannah Firmin. Without her gifted and magical artwork, this book could never have been written. Thank you, Hannah, for saying yes to my book project after just fifteen minutes on the phone with a total stranger and having never read one word of the manuscript. You've exceeded my expectations, and I look forward to more collaborations in the future.

My next words of appreciation go to my three editors, Sharon Faelten, Terry Allen, and Miranda Fisk. I am immensely grateful for both Terry and Sharon's fine understanding of the English language. They were ruthless in chopping off my long sentences and taught me to write with more clarity and succinctness. At the same time, they respected my need to write this book in my own voice. They both encouraged me to add more anecdotes and to speak from personal experience much more than I had originally planned.

High words of praise go to my talented graphic designer, Andrea Gray, who transformed my manuscript and Hannah's illustrations into such a charming work of art. Thank you, Andrea, for your understanding in working with me. As a new writer and self-publisher of my first book, I know I tried your patience on many occasions.

To Miranda Fisk, my content editor, I owe many words of thanks for keeping me on the straight and narrow. I deeply respect her commitment to the natural world and her undying devotion to protecting the native plants of our beloved New England. She was instrumental in my decision to rip out my newly planted petasites before it could take over our Vermont woodland. Thanks, Miranda, for your keen editing, for your patience in teaching me to be more ecologically responsible, and for your early gardening years at Muddy Creek during which I learned so much working at your side.

To my husband, Terry, I'd like to say that if it weren't for your love and support my book dream would never have become a reality. From the day we sat on our screened porch and I told you about my garden book idea, you have been my staunchest supporter. The fact that you believed in my project from its inception has instilled me with confidence and empowered me to lift my wings and fly. Thank you from the bottom of my heart for your generosity in financially backing my book. I hope that it will reap some profits, unlike our gardens which will probably be a money pit for the rest of our lives.

To Jared Gange, I owe deep gratitude for his generosity of spirit in sharing his writing and publishing knowledge. Jared introduced me to Andrea Gray and also directed me to Four Colour Imports, who did a masterful job in printing *Garden Notes from Muddy Creek.* I would not have known how to find these high quality people if it weren't for Jared. Thanks, Jared, for your encouraging words along the way.

Thanks to my daughter, Heather Mahoney, for her careful and thorough proof-reading. Heather earned a degree in horticulture from the University of Wisconsin, and is a master gardener. Heather, you were perfect for this book, and thank you for fitting it into your busy holiday schedule.

To all four daughters, Floery, Heather, Heidi and Shannon, thank you for your on-going interest in my project and for your understanding when my book consumed my time and energy and left me drained of my normal exuberance. Most of all, I want to thank each of you for standing by my side and never failing to believe in me.

To my special gardening buddy and dear friend, Robin Coleburn, I have nothing but the most heart-felt words of praise and appreciation. For the past three years, she has fielded frantic phone calls at all hours of the day. "What is the species name of your blackberry lily? Can I rush over and get your opinion on the latest art for the cover? When and how often do you prune your boxwood?" These are just a few of the questions Robin answered over the course of my writing this book. Thank you for never once making me feel as if I were taking up too much of your time or taking advantage of your extraordinary garden knowledge and artist's eye.

And last, but certainly not least, I want to thank my extended family of cherished friends whose keen interest in my book has buoyed me emotionally throughout its creation. Special love and thanks to Kathy and Hal DeHaven, two of my dearest friends. The two of you have been with me through thick and thin, and I'm not sure I'd be where I am now without having had your unconditional love and support.

Introduction

It seems inevitable that I was to find Muddy Creek. From childhood on, my happiest hours have been spent outdoors. As a ten year old, I loved hiding away in my very first garden, a tiny room created in the center of an ancient privet hedge.

My early summers were spent at my grandmother's cabin in the Catskill Mountains, and looking back, I have come to realize how much that influenced my life. One of my grandmother's many gifts to me was sharing her love of nature and all of its creations. She was always pointing out wildflowers on our walks and she kept a board propped in her little spring-fed pool to prevent frogs from drowning. To this day, I have vivid memories of Nana gently trapping wasps in her handkerchief and releasing them outdoors. Looking back on those formative years, I realize they nourished some deep need within me that I was unaware of at the time.

So one early spring day in 1996, when a young Realtor took Terry and me to a fallow, sorely neglected parcel of land in Ferrisburgh, I got goose bumps as soon as we began our walk. After making our way through burdock and cedar-infested farm fields and along the banks of little Muddy Creek, we arrived at a high clearing, sheltered to the north by woodlands and looking out on farmland and mountains to the south and east.

Terry and I silently looked at each other and knew that this was the beginning of the rest of our lives at Muddy Creek. We felt to the core that this land was meant to be ours, and that our search had ended on this spot. Terry turned to me and asked where we would site a house and I replied, "We are standing on it!" Within a few feet, give or take, we had been instinctively drawn to what would later prove to be the perfect site for our house. And, as we stood there and took in our good fortune, I innately knew that all my prior years had been leading to this incredible piece of Vermont upland and the stewardship that would come with it.

Over the next two years, we designed and built the house of our dreams, modeled after a two-hundred-year-old Vermont farmstead, complete with a recycled slate roof, old pine floors and stone garden walls. We had both lived in old houses all of our lives, but now we had the best of both worlds, a house that looked old but had modern plumbing and heating. It would be many years before we would have to worry about updating.

Finally, I could turn my thoughts to landscaping. Luckily, several people had recommended the same person, Andrea Morgante, of Site Works. Andrea was perfect for me. She had me write extensive lists of my favorite plants, shrubs and trees. We talked at length about the kind of atmosphere I wished to create in my gardens. But, I must admit that when she showed her first drawings to me, I had a difficult time embracing them. It wasn't that they weren't just what I had hoped for and dreamed of, but I felt as if I were undeserving of such professional and abundant gardens.

My mother was a bookish librarian and an indoor person. Her sole interest in gardening entailed planting a few hyacinths and tulips next to her patio chair to enjoy as she sat and read for hours. And like my mother, for most of my life I had never done more than dig a quick hole in the ground and plunk in a plant in the hopes that it would grow. So it took some serious talks with Terry and a few close friends before I was able to overcome my feelings of unworthiness and give Andrea the go-ahead. And go ahead she did, with great skill, gusto and dust flying everywhere, at the end of which she packed up her crew and left.

A great silence descended upon Muddy Creek, a silence that had not existed for two full years of house, barn and garden construction. All of a sudden, I was alone with these massive gardens and realized that I knew hardly anything about their maintenance and ongoing care. I thought back to when my husband had asked Andrea if I would be able to tend the gardens by myself and was reminded of her response to his question, "Terry, these are surely not one-caretaker gardens!"

Realizing I was in over my head, I called Andrea, who immediately sent Miranda Fisk, a delightful, hard-working young gardener to my rescue. For the next seven years, I worked alongside Miranda and several other knowledgeable gardeners, read endless garden books, and hung out with some of Vermont's finest perennial gardeners. Slowly and inexorably I became a gardener.

It seems that my life here at Muddy Creek has taken me full circle. From my simple beginnings as a child exploring and playing outdoors, and later, as an adult riding, biking or walking through some of the prettiest landscapes in the world, I have finally slowed my pace. The serene, natural beauty of my world here at Muddy Creek has seduced me into a quieter way of living. I am finally centered and know in my heart that I will spend the rest of my life and my creative energies here in my gardens surrounded by this magnificent Vermont landscape.

The idea for this book came as an epiphany a few summers after the gardens were installed. I suddenly realized that there must be vast numbers of gardeners who have inherited gardens, bought gardens full-blown, or like me, created them without much prior knowledge. I eagerly set about putting some thoughts on paper and gradually my envisioned book began to take shape.

Right from its inception, my main goal was to condense and simplify the immense subject of tending ornamental perennial gardens. Most of us lead busy lives, and I wanted to create an easy-to-read book that new gardeners could use as a guide in their early years of gardening.

I also envisioned that my book would be artistically beautiful as well. They say timing is everything in life, and such was the case with finding Hannah Firmin, my incredibly talented, English illustrator. After fifteen minutes of talking with me on the phone and having not read a word of my book, she agreed to come on board. Her charming block prints are exactly what I had envisioned for my book right from its inception. With Hannah as my talented and dedicated partner, the book slowly became a reality. I hope you enjoy it. It is the book I wish someone had given me when I was a new gardener.

Of all man's creations,
the garden is the greater perfection.

— Frank H. Cabot

JANUARY

Design Concepts and Thoughts

or many winters I gazed out our kitchen window at the wall of woods on the north side of our house. Years ago, our garden designer had placed large stone steps in the bank leading to this neglected woodland. But those enticing, algae-covered stones never led anywhere, and over the years I felt a growing urge to create a garden in those woods. This hidden place became my secret garden, and I alone knew of the wondrous treasures hidden there: an ancient chestnut oak, massive outcroppings of ledge, and a large native cherry tree under whose twisted, moss-covered trunk I sought solace if things weren't right with my world.

Not until Terry decided to build a small writing cabin further up in those woods was I given the impetus to share my hideaway. My mind began racing with all the design ideas I had been harboring for years. Every spare moment was spent figuring out how to bring into reality a garden that had existed only in my fantasies. I was determined to create this garden by myself, but I had little, if any, design experience. Along with my enthusiasm, I felt a large dose of anxiety.

Nevertheless, I forged ahead. During my years of tending our gardens, I've made some important changes to their original design. In doing so, I discovered that I possess latent design capabilities just begging to be put to use.

This chapter recounts how I transformed our overgrown, bramble-infested woodland into the garden I envisioned in my dreams. In the process, I learned that even though some projects have tentative beginnings, they often reap the most rewards.

BEGINNING THOUGHTS

Gardens are personal expressions. The best gardens reflect the spirit of the person or persons who made them. Gardeners who design for themselves tend to impart their own personality rather than a "design solution" on their gardens. So when trying your hand at design, try to start with a clear idea or understanding of what pleases you. Like most passionate gardeners, I spend many hours daydreaming about the changes I plan to make to the gardens. It seems as though I am always seeking a greater perfection. Terry keeps asking, "Are the gardens finished yet?" He is such an innocent. With all this land, endless visions of new gardens swirl in my head like dancing sugar plums on the night before Christmas.

Observe your site and be patient. Do not rush in until you have done your homework. Gardens work best when they are not an imposition on the landscape, but rather when they tease out its best attributes. There should be a complimentary relationship between the contrived landscape and the natural landscape. Gardens inspired from natural features enhance rather than overwhelm their surroundings. I became familiar with every bump and hollow in our woodland before taking out the chainsaws. I observed how sun, rain, wind and snowfall impacted our woods over several seasons. I also took note of areas that drained naturally as well as sections that remained perpetually dry or waterlogged. This background work allowed me to develop a clear, mental image of my project. As a result, when I finally put pencil to paper to create my design sketches, they flowed easily. No matter how crude your drawing skills are, it is invaluable to make these drawings. They serve to keep your design ideas on track and help you avoid getting caught up in small details. In the beginning stages of designing a garden space, it is important to stay focused on the big picture.

If possible, visit lots of gardens both near your home and during your travels. Frank Cabot's garden, "Les Quatre Vents," in Quebec, Canada, is one of my favorite gardens. It has been acclaimed as the most aesthetically satisfying and horticulturally exciting landscape experience in North America. This garden continues to remain in my mind because it offers a diversity of sensory experiences and intellectual stimulation, as well as humorous and whimsical surprises. Les Quatre Vents celebrates the purest of human pleasures, the making of a garden.

One of the great by-products of garden visits is the opportunity to plagiarize. To quote Frank Cabot, "Gardeners are plagiarists and the best gardeners are the best plagiarists." So feeling as if Frank gave me permission, I have stolen the idea behind one of his most enjoyable garden features. My version will involve a five-foot copper frog to be sculpted by one of my favorite Vermont artists, Eben Markowski, and placed in the grasses by our water pond. When visitors walk down the steps to the water's edge, they will trip a motion sensor which will cause the frog to burst into song. This project is still in the planning stages, but that is half the fun. I laugh out loud as I picture straw-hatted garden lovers dancing next to our frog as he belts out "Joy to the World" (by Three Dog Night).

History invariably plays a role when creating a garden. Every period of gardening throughout the ages has its relevance. It is simply impossible to ignore the influences of the past when planning a present-day garden. As a passionate gardener, I spend as much time as possible exploring other gardens, both public and private. I read as many garden books and magazines as I can lay my hands on. Each time I read something new or visit a garden, I accumulate fresh images and impressions which are stored (often on paper to assist my aging brain) for future reference. As a result, when my creative juices start to flow, this wealth of stored information becomes a valuable resource. (See the month of December for a list of the books which have given me the greatest delight and inspiration.)

Good garden design draws its inspiration from nature. Terry and I have been fortunate enough to walk through English woodlands in early springtime when they are thickly carpeted with masses of intermingled bluebells and white-flowering leeks. It's as if you have suddenly found yourself in a mystical land inhabited only by fairies. We are attempting to emulate those enchanting displays here in a bit of our woods. Having yet to see any sign of fairies at Muddy Creek, it will remain to be seen if our efforts pay off.

Successful gardens have a strong sense of place. As I took my first tentative steps to create our woodland garden, I realized that I have always been a place maker. So, it came as no surprise that my new garden has given me a strong connection to the woodlands of my youth. As a child, I felt safe and protected when playing in the woods. Mark Twain said, "Only people who never quite give up their childhood are living life to its fullest." Whenever I poke around in our wooded hillside looking at toadstool families, mosses aquiver with spore-dispersing chalices, and rotting stumps bejeweled with azure-blue lichen, I am transported back 50 years, and for a few precious moments I am a child again.

BASIC DESIGN CONCEPTS

Attractive gardens seldom just happen; they are designed. Well-thought-out designs ensure that gardens develop in a structured manner. One of the first things to figure out is what a new garden space means to you. Will it be formal with straight lines and a sense of order whose components form neat patterns? Or will it meander through a woodland or meadow allowing the natural landscape to dictate the design? Are you longing to create a space where you can quietly sit to contemplate a vista or fading sunset? Or do you wish to embellish an outside setting in which to gather family and friends for eating and conversing?

There should be three basic elements in your mind at the beginning of your design process. The first is unity. Even the simplest gardens need a sense of unity. This means that there should be a consistent theme throughout, with no jarring ingredients. The concept of unity is the most difficult of the three basic design elements, and amateur designers have to work hard to get it right in their first efforts. One of my pet peeves in this category is a lawn strewn with rocks or trees with little or no thought given to their placement. Often the rocks are a glaring white and the trees nondescript and of many different types. There is absolutely no unity whatsoever and the eye continually darts amongst these discordant objects. One well-placed rock with an overhanging tree would be a better solution and far more restful to the eyes.

Practicality is the second design element that needs strong consideration. Gardens should make sense and work well with their setting and with the users of the garden space. Also, they should fit the nature of the people who live within them. This is often the most difficult element for a professional designer to get right. Amateurs designing their own gardens have a better understanding of their goals and needs than outsiders. I had to dig up and move our entire boxwood garden inward by three feet after our professional designer had finished installing the gardens. She had intended for me to walk through this intricate garden every time I came out of our potting shed door. This made sense from a purely aesthetic standpoint, but it was simply not practical for me, who usually has an armful of garden tools and two rambunctious dogs in tow.

The last element of importance involves proportion. The major elements in successful garden spaces are always in proper scale with each other. Newly planted trees and shrubs take many years to reach maturity and it is important to place them so they can properly fill their allotted space in the long run. We have a small pagoda dogwood *(Cornus alternifolia)* next to our stone steps leading into

the woodland garden. Except for ground covers around it, it sits in a space too large for its present size. It takes all of my patience (which I have little of) to let it remain there unembellished. I have to remind myself that in just a few more years it will be exactly the right size for its space and will become a year-round focal point with its elegantly tiered branches, flowers and berries.

Having spent plenty of time contemplating your new garden (hopefully it wasn't as long as the seven years I spent dreaming of my woodland garden) you should be ready to put some basic design sketches on paper. Structure provides the bones of a garden and should constitute the framework when you make your first drawings. Some gardeners have a natural bent for design and can visualize things in their head as they study a space. I do this quite well myself and actually have difficulty visualizing two-dimensional drawings. But I still forced myself to make these basic drawings, knowing how easy it is to become distracted when working on a large project. These drawings do not need to be too detailed; simply sketch out the main structural elements of your overall scheme. As you delineate the shapes within your design, think of the whole space as a bulky, three-dimensional design. My sketches showed the location of the trees, shrubs and rocks that were to remain, as well as the ones I planned to add. Around each of these main elements, I denoted areas to be filled in with smaller plants and areas to be reserved for pathways.

No single element is as important as where you place paths. Paths provide a sense of direction and invite you into a garden.

It is important to know that the spaces between plantings are equally important as the plants themselves. This means that there should be a pleasing proportion of mass relative to empty space or voids. It is helpful for those of you who have taken art courses to think of these masses and voids as positive and negative spaces. Paths, terraces, stairways and lawns all fall into the void category, and as such should be kept in scale with the design. The creative process for surfaces such as paths and terraces takes almost as much energy as plant material because they act as a framework to the overall design.

The structural elements of a design are the most important and they strongly influence its character and style. When creating your structure, always make sure you leave or add elements for winter interest. My woodland garden is separated from our circular drive and vinca bank by a simple post and wire fence. In the

summer and early fall this fence is festooned with the yellow, bell-shaped flowers of the vine, *Clematis tangutica*. For the remainder of fall and throughout the winter, this same fence delights the eye with its winter blanket of downy seed heads. Not only does this fence provide a major structural element by separating two distinctly different garden spaces, it also provides year-round interest and adds an element of mystery to the partially hidden woodland.

In a small garden, a simple evergreen or a deciduous tree with interesting bark and shape can serve the dual purpose of acting as a main structural element, while adding beauty throughout the seasons. *Juniperus chinensis* 'Torulosa' (Juniper with bright green foliage and a twisted habit), *Stewartia pseudocamellia* (Japanese stewartia), Japanese maples, *Acer griseum* (paper-bark maple) and crab apples are some examples of trees in this category.

Whether you are working with just a few elements or an entire woodland, as was my case, there are some basic principles to keep in mind. Trees give unity to a design and create a restful atmosphere. However, not all trees are the same in this respect. Conifers lend a staccato feeling to a garden, which in turn imparts an aura of stability. A row of tall, cypress trees standing watch on an Italian hilltop is a perfect example of the grounding effect of conifers. On the other hand, deciduous trees have the opposite affect. Their spreading branches and open leaf patterns give a feeling of movement and airiness. In woodland gardens, it is best when deciduous trees dominate so that light and air can filter in and flow freely around the garden. Try to get your choice of trees and shrubs right in the beginning stages of a project to eliminate any problems further down the road. Be especially careful when taking down mature trees because a site can be altered for a lifetime once a large tree has been removed.

Gardens are comprised of shapes, and in most gardens these shapes consist of a single or series of rectangular, diagonal or circular spaces. The strong lines of a chosen geometrical shape serve to guide designers when adding or retaining key structural elements to a new garden. This strong sense of architecture gives the eyes and mind a visual grounding. Two exceptions are woodland and meadow gardens where nature has already done most of the work. These are the easiest gardens to create because their design is governed by the natural lay of the land and not by geometrical patterns.

It takes a greater level of creativity and experience to design a garden on a bare plot of land. Open spaces involve the establishment of perimeters and structure, which can consume lots of money and take years to reach acceptable levels of maturity. If these are issues for you, try staggering the work and cost over a few years' time. A few attractive posts placed along a perimeter with wire strung between them can be used in several ways. The simplest and cheapest choice is to allow vines such as honeysuckle or clematis to turn the posts and wire into a living fence, just as I did at the top of my vinca bank. A more elegant solution involves the use of wooden trellises or wire frameworks to train (espalier) shrubs or trees to grow along a single plane. My friend Robin has espaliered a row of beech trees to separate the conifer garden behind her painting studio from the apple orchard beyond. Beech trees are especially beautiful as a living fence because they retain their pale, parchment-brown leaves in the winter, adding an ethereal touch to the winter landscape.

The key with any of these structural elements is to use sturdy materials, whether they consist of bricks, stone, wood, metal or plant material. The idea is to construct something that gives a sense of permanence and stability while providing privacy and protection from the outside world. Even small pieces of fencing used as accents or focal points within a garden's interior should be constructed of good materials. Flimsy, poorly wrought elements detract rather than enhance.

Gardens can easily be expanded into a meadow by using hedges, walls or a few well placed trees as border plantings to create a visual boundary between the controlled landscape and the natural one. Paths cut through tall meadow grasses and wild flowers catch the eye and entice you to explore the outer, wild garden. Something as costly and elegant as a gazebo or as simple as a single tree can be used as a focal point to draw your eye and encourage you to wander and discover what lies ahead.

Once you have determined the main structural elements, focal points should be created to attract attention to certain features or to add areas of interest to the garden. They act as eye-catchers or punctuation marks in a garden. Look for natural focal points, then go on to create some of your own or embellish the ones you have. The chestnut oak and twisted cherry were the beginning two focal points in our woodland. By placing a substantial piece of sculpture beneath the oak, an extra layer of richness and complexity was added to an already stunning feature.

In a small garden, it might be a piece of Italian pottery, a single American redbud planted in a bed of bergenia and candelabra primroses, or a Japanese maple under-planted with ferns to give the affect of an extended woodland. Zen Buddhists believe that the entire universe can be experienced in a lone tree or rock or bit of raked sand. I love Japanese gardens for exactly that reason. They fill me with a sense of order and magnitude and my daily cares seem inconsequential in comparison.

A good garden does not reveal all of its treasures at first glance.

In large gardens, a focal point might be as simple as a view into or out of the garden or as complicated as a large sculpture like our life-size lady leaping for joy under our chestnut oak. A well-placed piece of sculpture is one of the best ways to catch the attention of visitors and to draw them into a garden. Our one-of-a-kind copper sculpture was created by Eben Markowski (fathen@adelphia.net), a young Vermont metal sculptor who is well on his way to national recognition. He specializes in animals of all descriptions and his realistic style melds perfectly with the blue, green, purple, red and golden tones that burnish copper when exposed to the outside elements. A few years ago, Eben exhibited a life-size giraffe sculpture on the lawn of our art gallery. It was so startling to spot a giraffe here in Vermont that many passing cars came to a screeching halt. It was a great show stopper.

I regularly visit salvage companies to find things for our gardens. A pair of faded-green iron gates serves as an entry way to our woodland garden. In late spring they are clothed with the pale yellow blossoms of *Clematis* 'Guernsey Cream' while the scent of sweet woodruff perfumes their feet.

There are endless ways to add unique and interesting details to a garden. Even a small section of iron fencing placed in just the right spot can lift a garden out of the ordinary. But be careful not to clutter a garden space with too many accents. If these are overdone, you can create a muddled effect and cause a dis-

cordant feeling in the same manner as the poorly used rocks and trees talked about earlier in this chapter.

The best gardens have interesting elements throughout. They need not be as elaborate as Frank Cabot's musical frogs or swinging bridges. A friend recently brought me a small, concrete chimp called Max as a house gift. I placed him at the base of a small tree in my woodland garden where he sits laughing in delight as he scratches his bottom. I have a close-up view of him whenever I sit on my garden bench, and he never ceases to make me laugh. I can also see our elegant, copper lady from this same spot. I deliberately placed these two entirely different art objects in juxtaposition with each other to remind me to keep my sense of humor. Gardens can be fun, and my favorite gardeners are those who refuse to take themselves too seriously. When Mother Nature inevitably wreaks havoc on our efforts, it helps to be able to laugh at our temporal efforts of control.

Rocks and streams can be featured alone, but they work best when they are part of an overall design scheme. I used a number of craggy, moss-coated rocks as accents in our woodland garden. The trick was to make the rocks seem as if they had always been there. I kept moving and turning each rock until it was situated just right. Visitors never guess that these rocks were not there naturally and that we brought in large equipment to move and position each one. One of my favorites is embedded just below our ancient cherry and is surrounded by plantings of filipendula (meadowsweet), thalictrum (meadow rue), hostas, an overhanging aronia (chokeberry), hellebores, primroses, and masses of ferns and sedges.

Water features make great focal points. Water enlivens a garden and refreshes the spirit. Flowing water in even the simplest form, such as a solitary pot overflowing into a basin below, adds a sensory element to a garden. Our stream garden was created by embellishing a swale which had been eroded over the years by melting snow and torrential rains. One year, I pulled on my tall wellies and used a shovel to dig out masses of mucky soil from within the flow line of the spring torrents. By following the natural curves of the small stream and not imposing my will on it, my newly dug stream channel retained its natural beauty. I then lined it with strips of window screening and dumped in loads of small, gravelly stones to serve as the stream bed. And even though the stream bed is dry three-quarters of the year, it still gives the effect of a natural stream and waterway.

The banks of this garden had been planted years ago with structural trees and shrubs which included *Ilix verticillata* (winterberry), *Pinus mugo* (mugo pine), *Betula nigra* (river birch), hamamelis (witch hazel) and masses of elegant grasses. So, I was now afforded the luxury of focusing on smaler plants and shrubs as the final embellishment. I chose to add Joe-Pye weed, *Salix purpurea* 'Harmony' (variegated blue willow), *Rheum palmatum* 'Atrosanguineum' (ornamental rhubarb), ligularia, Siberian iris, self-sowing belamcanda (blackberry lily), and *Miscanthus sinensis* 'Zebrinus' (zebra grass). I dug gobs of wild forget-me-nots out of a nearby stream as a finishing touch. I am totally enchanted when delicate flowers such as forget-me-nots and self-sowing wild geranium and corydalis squeeze themselves into every inch of available ground. It is almost September as I write this and the forget-me-nots are still flaunting their heavenly blue flowers amongst the ornamental sweet potato, nicotiana, and coleus.

Each year, I add tropical plants to this garden to attempt to emulate the exotic gardens I've fallen in love with in southern England. Christopher Lloyd, one of my English gurus, was a major influence in giving me the courage to use exotic plantings. Besides owning and overseeing his gardens at Great Dixter in East Sussex, England, he is a world renowned garden writer and lecturer. His writings and exotic plantings at Great Dixter (I have yet to visit his gardens in person) have given me the courage to try some of his bold plant combinations here at Muddy Creek. He believes that exotics lift a garden out of the ordinary when intermingled with perennials in border plantings or large beds. I couldn't agree more. As a result, canna lilies, banana plants, *Brugmansia* x *candida* (angel's trumpet), *Ricinus communis* (castor bean), *Mina lobata* and many other exotic plants now add their tropical charms to my stream garden. When the eight-foot brugmansia is dripping in yellow trumpet-shaped flowers, the canna is aglow with its apricot-skinned blossoms, and the mina's exotic red and yellow flowers are entwined with the *Verbena bonariensis,* I feel a deep connection to my English mentor. Even though I must lug my huge brugmansia to a friend's greenhouse each fall and buy all new exotic plants from her each spring, it is so worth the effort. Thank you, Christo, for inspiring me with your passion, innovative thinking, and fearless plantsmanship. Terry and I plan to visit Great Dixter on our next trip to England. Perhaps we'll have the good fortune to share a pot of tea with you and Fergus.

PLANTING THOUGHTS

My first on-site task was to clear out masses of trees, shrubs and undergrowth in order to create a clean palette. When Beth Chatto, the famous English plantswoman cleared her woods to create a garden, she likened the newly opened woodland to a cathedral. As we cleared trees and masses of invasive plants such as buckthorn, honeysuckle and wild raspberries here at Muddy Creek, I kept thinking of Beth's metaphor, and it gave me the heart to keep on chopping. As the bare bones of the magnificent *Quercus prinus* (chestnut oak), the twisted cherry and the remaining maples, oaks, pines, birches and hemlocks revealed themselves, I could almost hear sighs of relief as they were released into the air and sunlight.

They were now free to stretch sideways and fill out. I will note here that these maples had grown tall canopies in order to reach the only available light in our dense woodland. So I was able to leave a chosen few because their extra tall canopies would allow plenty of light to reach any new plantings placed beneath them. Otherwise, maple trees work best when used as specimen trees on a lawn or in vast landscape gardens. Very few plants can grow under the dark, dense canopy of a mature maple. (Our buckthorn seems to be an exception.)

Once you have a concrete idea of how your new garden will look overall, you can start to choose specific plants. The layout of the design now becomes the vessel to be filled. As a self-taught garden designer, I will pass on some planting concepts and ideas that make sense to me from my readings, observations, and trials and errors. I believe that all my years of roaming the outdoors and observing the natural world have given me an advantage over people who have spent the majority of their time indoors. Also, my many years of submerging myself in every aspect of caring for our perennial gardens here at Muddy Creek seem to have given me a feeling of confidence that other new gardeners may not possess. So the following thoughts, suggestions and ideas are taken partly from the experts, but quite a few of my comments in this section come from personal observation and experience.

As your garden develops, be aware that it may take a few years to work it out to your satisfaction. Good gardens are continually evolving, and very few amateurs get things right on the first go-round. Be prepared to move plants around until you achieve the effects you are looking for. However, do try to get the large shrubs and trees situated correctly during the initial planting. It is costly and hazardous to move them once they are established.

Try to envision the basic arrangement and style of plants from the beginning. It is not important to make lists of individual plants, but do try to get a feeling for the atmosphere you wish to create. Be careful not to get too wrapped up in the details of these smaller plants until the structural parts of your garden have been installed and all the prep work on the soil has been completed. I brought in copious amounts of compost to enrich the soil and filled the paths with endless wheelbarrow loads of wood chips before I began the planting stage.

I found it easier as a beginning designer to not worry about which category of design a plant fits into. The basic idea is to figure out which plants will achieve

the affects you are looking for. *Also, this is the time to remember how important it is to "grow the right plant in the right place."* My early observations of our site allowed me to place dry-loving plants, wet-loving plants, and all the in-between plants in areas of the woodland garden that best suited their needs. As a result, I have lost very few plants and have saved a lot of stress for both the plants and myself. If you are not familiar with a wide range of plants, there are a number of books listed in my reference section which have extensive lists of plants and how to grow and use each one successfully.

Our woods already had lots of naturally occurring ground covers such as Canada mayflower (wild lily-of-the-valley), false Solomon's seal, corydalis, wild columbine, wood anemone, wild geranium, trout lily, hepatica and masses of violets, ferns, mosses, sedges and rushes. I spent lots of time studying the way these plants grew naturally in order to make my additions to the garden look as if they had always been there. I believe that there is no better way to plant than to follow the example set by nature. I added tall, feathery plants, such as cimicifuga (bug bane), Jacob's ladder, thalictrum (Japanese meadow rue) and *Rubus odoratus* (flowering raspberry) to catch the breezes and lighten up the forest floor. The tall trees were grounded with under-story trees and shrubs such as *Cornus mas* 'Golden Glory' (Cornelian cherry dogwood), magnolias, hornbeam, nine bark, enkianthus, fothergilla, rhododendron, azalea, clethra, mountain laurel, chokeberry, *Ilex verticillata* (winterberry), and witch hazel. Clematis, akebia and climbing hydrangea vines were planted to entwine fences and gates and wend their way up tree trunks.

Once I had planted the under-story to the large trees in our woodland, I followed Frank Cabot's line of thinking when it came to choosing the smallest plants. When he first started planting his woodland garden at "Les Quatre Vents," he bought every shade-loving plant he could lay his hands on. So last spring,

my friend Robin and I timed a trip to one of our favorite nurseries to coincide with the arrival of a new shipment of shade plants. Not only did I buy masses of plants which I had on my list, but I came home with new plants which I was not previously familiar with, such as *Diphylleia cymosa* (umbrella leaf), *Porteranthus trifoliatus* (Bowman's root), which is covered in May and June with white, star-shaped flowers on wiry red branches, jeffersonia, and *Bergenia* "Tubby Andrews", a bergenia with variegated leaves which re-blooms in late summer. We did try to leave some plants for other folks, but I'm afraid we took more than our share. My only excuse is that the woodland garden is so big that I needed copious amounts of plant material to fill up vast areas of bare soil.

I would like to pass on a great planting tip I learned from my daughter Heather and her friend Willy a few years back. I asked the two of them how they managed to create such a stunning arrangement of perennial plants in their stream garden. It is one of the most successful groupings of plants that I've seen here in Vermont. It is brimming with large-leaved plants of all descriptions, textures and sizes, each with unique leaves, flowers and seed heads. This magnificent bed of plants adorns a small waterway as it wends downward to a perfect pool at the bottom. They told me that they go to a nursery and pick out a group of plants that they not only love but that also look good together. Then they go home and plant them in one designated space. They repeat this over several buying trips until they have filled a complete bed in this manner. It's almost as if they are creating a patchwork quilt, with each "planting square" complimenting the surrounding ones. Heather makes exquisite quilts and Willy is an avid collector of art from all over the world, so I'm certain it is their combined artistic bents which keep them from creating a mish-mash.

In the final planting stage of my woodland garden, I used this same method to get me started. I had vast areas which needed planting, but my plant purchasing fund had been seriously depleted by the cost of the larger trees and shrubs. So, each time I visited a nursery, I would arrange a small group of plants just as if I were going to plant them then and there. I would then go home and put them in a space where they would be most visible, either along one of my paths or around a tree or rock. This gave me the most impact for the dollars spent because these densely planted areas gave the appearance of a garden well on its way to maturity. My favorite area planted in this manner is the series of cedar log steps rising up the hillside below the great oak. Brunera, bergenia, astilbe, ascarum (wild ginger), primroses, *Cornus candensis* (bunchberry), pachysandra, violets, tiarella, anemonella, and ferns of all descriptions have interwoven and fashioned themselves into a lush, living tapestry.

Even though I followed very few rules in creating our woodland garden, I would like to comment on one design rule that I like to follow. In large beds or a single extensive garden like our woodland, it works well to plant the same species of plants in repetitive masses around the garden. This method of planting gives a strong sense of unity and also creates a style of its own. Ground covers also look best when planted in mass because it causes the visual impact to come from the group as a whole. *This theory helps to avoid the pitfall of planting too many varieties of closely related species around a garden like a bad case of the measles.*

The best gardens have harmonious colors throughout the entire growing season. Many design plans start with far too many color combinations. Color should complement a design and not be an end in itself. Even single beds are most effective when planted with masses of plants that repeat themselves. Remember to think of green as a color also, from pale, spring greens, to the dark, heavy greens of summertime, to variegated leaves of all descriptions.

Another effective way of using color is to infuse several colors into a large group of same-species plants. I have masses of pink coneflowers growing in a small Victorian birdbath garden. Each year I intermingle tall zinnias in tones from pale apricot to hot pink to crimson among my single species of pink coneflower. Tall hyssop plants weave their way through the middle of the bed refreshing the palette with their cool blue flowers. This little garden is not jarring to my eye like the riotous colors of an English cottage garden, but I still refer to it as my "hot garden." I also think this garden works well because it is very small. Success often depends upon the scale you are working with.

Plants should be situated to be noticed and appreciated at different times of the year. In my woodland garden, I have planted groups of bulbs along the pathways where they can easily be seen. If I scattered them throughout the whole of the garden, they would have little visual impact until years down the road. I will continue to add bulbs each fall in order to have a bigger show as the years go on. Perhaps some day it truly will feel as if fairies have come to inhabit our woods, just like in England.

The right time to do a job is when you
have the time to do it properly.
— CHRISTOPHER LLOYD

FEBRUARY

Pruning

ardening chores in February are one of the highlights of my year. During this month, time moves more slowly as the slumbering natural world enfolds Muddy Creek in a peaceful aura. On the days I venture outside to prune, the crisp, winter air invigorates me. I seem alone in the world as I quietly study the stark beauty of our winter landscape. For all these reasons and because there are virtually no other chores to worry about, February is a perfect time to prune.

As a result of my years as the main gardener at Muddy Creek, I have leaned how important regular pruning is to the success and health of our gardens. And having inherited my Swiss father's compulsion for neatness, I embrace the mantra of British gardener Christopher Lloyd: "Plants' growth can be anticipated, intercepted and shaped according to a gardener's will and temperament." I am certain that some of the joy I experience while pruning is due to of this brief sense of control.

This chapter's goal is to simplify the daunting, confusing and often mystifying elements of pruning. It is my hope that these February pages will clarify and shed some light on this subject. They are meant to serve as a general guide to pruning the more familiar garden plants. For pruning unusual, more complicated plants, I recommend consulting my resource list at the back of this book. Try not to be intimidated, though. It is almost impossible to kill a plant by incorrect pruning. In the long run, most plants benefit immensely from a good chopping back.

REASONS TO PRUNE

Although a number of woody plants need minimal pruning, the majority benefit immensely from regular pruning. Neglected shrubs and trees often contain dying or dead wood which makes them vulnerable to weather, disease and all types of insects. On the other hand, woody plants kept open and airy are less prone to attack because bugs and disease have a proclivity for dark, dank places. To promote health in all your shrubs and trees, remove any dead, diseased, crossed, or weak branches on a regular basis. Sickly branches are prone to breaking or ripping in strong windstorms. It is important to keep trees properly pruned from a young age.

Regular pruning reinvigorates plants by directing energy back to the roots, which then send up new, healthy wood to replace the old, worn-out material. One has only to cut back a *Salix integra* 'Hakuro Nishiki' (variegated Japanese willow) or a *Cornus alba* (red-barked dogwood) to 8 inches or so in late winter or early spring to witness the exquisite color of the new stems and leaves of these colorful shrubs. Lilacs are another example of how restorative the removal of old wood is to vitality as shrubs age. By cutting away one-third of the oldest branches of a lilac shrub, you stimulate a fresh burst of energy directly to the roots. The roots then respond by growing new shoots to replace the old, worn-out ones.

Another primary reason to prune is to stimulate and control flower or fruit formation. This aspect of pruning is an immense subject and runs the gamut from fruit growers pruning for optimal harvest yields to Japanese gardeners forcing mums to flower according to precise garden designs. (This book is only concerned with ornamental perennial plants and does not discuss plants grown for edible fruit.)

The final reason to prune is to shape all woody plants to suit garden size, design and personal taste. The shapes and sizes of garden shrubs and trees are key determinants in setting the overall tone in perennial gardens. It is important

to keep plants in scale with your garden size and design. It may take a few years to decide what works best for you. You will need to know whether you prefer a formal or informal look or, if your gardens are expansive, a combination of the two. Small gardens created by city dwellers are often controlled and clipped, while English cottage gardens tend to be wild and rambling. The key is to develop a garden style which best suits your personal aesthetic, physical space and way of life. There are no hard rules for this type of pruning.

I have put off until July all discussions of summertime pruning chores for herbaceous, non-woody perennials. Many people don't think of deadheading or pinching back as more than tidying up the garden, but in reality they are very important types of pruning, so I have chosen to devote an entire chapter to summertime pruning.

PRUNING

A great deal of pruning is based on common sense and becomes second nature once you have some hands-on experience. Top gardeners seem to have an innate ability to look at a plant and know how to prune it. But these talented folks often find it difficult to pass this ability on to new gardeners.

Pruning is complex, due to the many variables involved. First of all, pruning is very "species specific." In order to prune properly, it is often essential to know the species you are working with, especially if a plant happens to fall within a pruning gray area. A large percentage of woody perennials do not fit neatly into the two basic pruning categories: Dormant season pruning, for plants that bloom on current season's growth, and growing season pruning, for plants that produce flowers on old wood. For instance, some species in the hydrangea genus differ greatly regarding pruning times even though they all bloom in the summertime. The clematis genus is usually separated into three pruning categories because some species bloom on old wood, others on new wood, while plants in the third group bloom on a combination of old and new wood. Other factors such as the age and health of a plant, climate, and even soil fertility can all play roles in determining when and how to prune.

All of these factors make for much confusion in the minds of new gardeners. Sometimes two gardeners will ask the same question about how and when to prune an identical species of plant and get entirely different answers. So much

depends on the above factors as well as an individual gardener's personal goals. The following pages attempt to simplify and demystify the most confusing elements surrounding this all-important garden practice. The benefits derived from regular pruning are countless, and properly carried out, pruning goes a long way towards maintaining year-round health and beauty in perennial gardens. To neglect these tasks can spell disaster in so many ways.

PRINCIPLES OF PLANT GROWTH

Most gardeners can acquire adequate pruning skills by learning some fundamentals of plant physiology. The basic principles are really quite simple, and once understood, should give a gardener the confidence to prune successfully.

All plant growth is predetermined; pruning merely directs and augments the inevitable. Each plant species grows according to its specific genetic makeup.

The main principle that governs and directs all plant growth is that of Apical Dominance. Stated simply, the premise of this principle is that the terminal bud at the apex of the leader branch of a shrub or tree dominates and suppresses all other buds. Further, the lateral buds close to the tip of each branch stay dormant, allowing terminal buds to grow without the close interference from side branches. Plant hormones govern bud growth and play a key role in determining a plant's branching pattern. Thus, when a plant is pruned, hormones spring into action, sending new signals telling the plant where to redirect its growth.

CUTTING TECHNIQUES

When pruning, always cut no more than a quarter of an inch above an outgrowing stem, eye or growth bud. Try to angle the cut so it slopes down and away from the bud, allowing the moisture to drain. Cutting too close to the bud or too high above can damage the branch. Any excess tissue will die back and become a site for attack by disease or pests.

Rule: The terminal bud is the first to grow in the spring.
This results in an orderly and controlled rate of growth and
gives each species of plant its character and shape.

Branch collars contain protective chemicals which assist wounds in the healing process and repel decay organisms. Modern day horticulturists advocate letting these chemicals heal wounds naturally rather than applying man-made healing salves. For those reasons, always sever a branch from the trunk of a tree at the outer edge of the branch collar. For a branch small enough to hold so it doesn't fall while cutting, use a small pruning saw. For larger branches, cut in a three-step manner as shown in the diagram, to avoid damaging or ripping the protective branch collar.

It is best to keep all tools sharp and clean by using a whetstone and dipping them in a 10% bleach solution or rubbing alcohol (if working with diseased plants). This takes very little time but goes a long way toward preventing torn plant tissue and possible attack by disease or pests.

Conifers: Most conifers rarely produce new growth from a cut made below the green on a branch. It is important to either prune above the leafy part or remove the entire branch. To control plant size from a young age, regularly snip back new growth tips at the end of each branch you wish to keep in check.

PRUNING METHODS

Thinning: *This type of pruning involves cutting off a stem or branch at its point of origin on the parent branch or where a branch forms a Y at a crotch.*

Most horticulturalists recommend this method of pruning as the best way to control growth while also maintaining the original shape of a shrub or tree.

Pruning by thinning allows more air and light to reach interior spaces and is therefore a major pest and disease deterrent. It also allows photosynthesis to occur to its fullest potential which, in turn, provides maximum energy for growth. This method of pruning has the added advantage of not stimulating unnecessary new growth.

Heading: *A branch is headed when it is cut back to a stub, lateral bud, or smaller-diameter lateral branch.*

Pruning in this manner causes a loss of apical dominance due to the removal of the terminal bud on that section of the shrub or tree. As a result, vigorous side shoots develop from lateral buds directly below the cut, while buds lower down on the branch remain inhibited. This pruning method is the best way to promote a bushy habit in a lanky shrub or tree. Fruit growers often head trees to promote branching on sparse limbs.

Shearing: *This is a specialized form of pruning which involves removing the terminal buds on virtually all the stems or tips of a plant.*

Shearing creates a bonanza of new growth directly below the cuts, which results in a dense canopy of exterior leaves. Shearing is most often reserved for hedge shrubs or topiary where a formal look is the gardener's goal. In theory, this method of pruning is similar to heading in that it only involves cutting back short lengths of top growth. However, most shrubs and trees are not suited for shearing

and would wear out from having to produce so many extra tips. When shearing hedges, try to trim on a slant to create a wide base at the bottom of the hedge. The narrower top allows sunlight to reach the lower portion of the hedge.

Pinching, Deadheading and Cutting Back: *These important types of late-spring and summertime pruning are discussed at length in the month of July.*

WHEN TO PRUNE WHAT?
THAT IS THE QUESTION

Dormant Season Pruning

The dormant season (months plants are not actively growing) is the correct time to prune most summer blooming plants (plants that bloom in early June through summer). New wood will not have grown yet, and therefore no flower buds will have set. Summer blooming shrubs and trees almost always bloom on the current season's growth (new wood that grew and set flower buds after the end of the dormant period). However, there are some exceptions to this rule. Some hydrangea species flower on old wood (wood that grew the previous season) even though they bloom in the summer. There is more information on hydrangeas later in this chapter. It is important to know if you have plants that do not conform to the rules.

In general, it is best to prune woody plants in this category just before new growth starts in the spring or buds begin to swell. This would be late winter to early spring, or whenever these conditions occur in your garden zone. Pruning in the fall is less desirable because some of the plant's energy stores may still be in the leaves and branches and because new growth may be stimulated at the wrong time of year.

A major plus for pruning during the dormant season is that it is beneficial to the gardener as well as to plants. It is so much easier to examine the structure of a woody plant while it is lacking leaves. Also, there are virtually no other garden chores to demand your time, so pruning offers the perfect excuse to venture outside on a mild, late-winter or early-spring day.

Pruning during this period also promotes better healing than at other times of the year. Wounds lose less sap and callus over more quickly during this period when their energy reserves aren't needed for growth. Therefore, diseases are less likely to infect pruning wounds. However, try to carry out these tasks when you think temperatures will stay above freezing for a few days to avoid damaging tender, exposed plant tissue.

This is also the best time for any heavy shaping and cutting back of plants which have outgrown their allotted garden space. Try to follow the one-third rule — that is, remove no more than a third of a woody plant's stems or branches any one year.

Growing Season Pruning

The other main type of pruning is carried out during the active growing season (that is, from spring bud swell through leaf drop in the fall). This type involves most of the spring-flowering plants which flower from buds set on the previous year's growth — in other words, old wood.

It is best to prune plants that flower on old wood immediately after their blossoms fall and before new leaves have fully expanded. A harmful dwarfing effect can result in a shrub or tree if it is pruned right after its leaves have developed.

Growing-season pruning also includes removing water sprouts and suckers that often develop as a result of earlier, dormant-season pruning. Wisteria vines,

which need severe, dormant-season pruning (cutting all side branches back to a few spurs) are notorious for producing suckers throughout the summer. It is important to remove these on a regular basis in order to keep the plant under control and to direct the plant's energy back to the main vine.

Hedge shrubs, such as privet and boxwood, maintain their shape best when they are pruned several times during the growing season. The main trimming and shaping should be done early in the season followed by light tidying a few times throughout the summer. It is a good idea to prune hedges during a period of cloudy, cool weather to avoid sunburn on newly exposed leaves.

The following list gives specific pruning information for woody shrubs and small trees most commonly found in temperate garden regions. In my early garden years, I often went from one garden book to the next in search of the correct pruning information for my woody plants. Eventually, I created my own pruning charts, and they have saved me many hours of wasted time. With this list close at hand, I spend more time pruning and less time looking things up. As a result, I now prune with more confidence and rarely have to consult a book. With practice, pruning can become second nature to you, as well.

Rule: Give plants three months of active growing time (months when leaves are dropping or the plant is dormant do not count) between the time you prune and when they come into bloom.

PRUNING GUIDELINES FOR SPRING-FLOWERING WOODY PERENNIALS

Plants in this category should be pruned during the growing season as soon as possible after flowering and preferably before leafburst.

Azalea: Refer to rhododendron

Cercis (redbud): These small trees need very little pruning except for the standard pruning to remove dead, diseased or crossed wood. However, I periodically remove drooping branches from the two redbuds planted in the middle of our circular driveway. This lightens up the trees and allows views through this garden to the surrounding lawns and gardens.

Chaenomeles (flowering quince): Quince does not respond well to heavy pruning. However, if size is an issue, a few stems can be removed.

Cornus (dogwood): Some of these species should have up to a quarter of their oldest stems removed each year. To maintain the vivid red-colored stems of red-barked dogwoods such as *Cornus alba* or the greenish yellow stems of *Cornus stolonifera,* do a complete renewal pruning every 7 to 10 years or whenever they lose their color.

Deutzia: In areas with harsh winters, this plant can suffer from winterkill. In early spring, remove all dead wood and reshape the plant, thinning if the plant has gotten too out of control.

Fothergilla: This shrub hardly ever needs any pruning other than the removal of dead, diseased or crossed wood.

Forsythia: Try to remove one-third of the oldest canes each year right down to the ground, unless you have plenty of room and want to let it ramble, as in a hedge row.

Hypericum (St. John's-wort): Prune only for normal maintenance or when shaping is required.

Kalmia latifolia **(mountain laurel):** Needs little pruning, but the removal of spent flowers may promote better flowering the following season.

Kerria: Each year thin and remove all winterkill. Kerria responds well to a hard cut-back each year.

Kolkwitzia amabilis **(beauty bush):** To maintain vigor, remove oldest branches to ground level each year.

Lindera (spice bush): This shrub benefits from a hard, regenerative pruning every few years.

Magnolia: Each year, remove any dead or diseased wood immediately after flowering. Otherwise, magnolia shrubs require little pruning other than shaping to meet your personal aesthetic.

Malus species (crab apple): This wide group of small trees require little pruning except to remove dead, diseased or crossed branches each year. However, in the ornamental garden, more extensive pruning is often done to accentuate the interesting bark and branching patterns inherent to crab apple trees.

Philadelphus (mock orange): Unless pruned annually to promote bushiness, these plants can become leggy and unattractive.

Pieris: This elegant shade shrub needs only the removal of dead or diseased wood to maintain its shape. However, the removal of the spent flowers may promote better flowering the following season.

Prunus (floral species such as choke cherry, blackthorn, and cherry laurel): In early years, prune these shrubs to shape, and thereafter prune to control size and health. Always make clean cuts and avoid damage to branch collars.

Rhododendron (this genus includes evergreen and deciduous azaleas): Old, leggy plants can be rejuvenated by cutting them back by one half after flowering in the spring or before new flower buds begin to form in mid-summer. However, this genus of plants can be left to its own devices, especially in woodland gardens, which allows plants to exhibit their natural, graceful growth patterns. Deadheading after flowering can promote more blossoms the next season, while pinching out the terminal buds on branches stimulates bushier plants.

Rhus (sumac): Sumacs need little care but can be kept in size by a rejuvenative pruning every few years.

Salix (willow): Small willow shrubs and trees need to be pruned on a regular basis to keep them in shape and within their allotted garden space. For willows with variegated leaves, such as *Salix integra* 'Hakuro Nishiki', a yearly pruning back to six to eight inches from the ground restores the pinkish, green, and white leaves which characterize this Japanese cultivar.

Scotch Broom: In the perennial garden, these shrubs maintain a tidier appearance if they are pruned after flowering in early June; otherwise they can become very scraggly and unkempt.

Syringa (lilac): Mature lilacs greatly benefit from a yearly, restorative pruning. Each spring, as soon as possible after flowering, remove two or three of the oldest branches all the way to the ground or to a low crotch near ground level. This annual thinning not only keeps older lilacs in bounds, but also promotes health and flowering.

Viburnum: This large group of spring-flowering shrubs needs little pruning to maintain their stately shape. Periodically thin out old wood and canes to control size and shape on taller species.

Weigela: These shrubs are prone to die-back in colder regions and should be removed of their winterkilled branches in the dormant season. It is best to reshape a badly affected plant at the same time the dead wood is removed. You will lose some of the present season's blooms, but you will promote health in a damaged plant. If your weigelas come through winter unscathed, then it is only necessary to prune to shape the shrub following its spring flowering period.

PRUNING GUIDELINES FOR
SUMMER-FLOWERING WOODY PERENNIALS

This group of plants flower on new wood and should be pruned in the dormant season, preferably in late winter or early spring. The optimal time is just before new growth or buds begin to swell, whenever that occurs in your garden zone.

Aesculus parviflora (bottlebrush buckeye): This shrub is in the horse chestnut family and needs very little pruning. However, selective pruning can be done in the dormant season to restrict its size.

Buddleia (butterfly bush): In regions with harsh winters, some gardeners cut their buddleia to within a few inches of the crown in the fall and cover them with straw to protect the roots. Otherwise, in early spring or late winter, cut plants back to just above two or more new buds near ground level on the old wood. In milder regions, buddleias exhibit strong buds further up on their stems and should be cut back to just above those buds.

Calycanthus floridus (**sweet shrub or Carolina allspice**): Prune in late winter or early spring, and periodically do a renewal pruning if a plant becomes too leggy or overgrown.

Cephalanthus occidentalis (**buttonbush**): This shrub only requires maintenance pruning but can be severely cut back close to the ground if it outgrows its space or becomes too unkempt.

Clethra: Clethra needs little pruning and actually may lose a few years of bloom if cut back too harshly. Last winter, I found this out firsthand when rabbits or small rodents chopped off the tops of five, newly planted clethra under our pergola. The plants rebounded nicely and came back with strong leaf and branch growth, but I was robbed of every one of their soft-pink flower clusters which normally grace our front patio in the summer.

Cotinus coggygria (**smokebush**): If you wish to keep this shrub in its space and are mostly interested in its beautiful leaf color, then remove or cut back the oldest stems each spring. However, it you want it to grow large and exhibit the smoky flower heads it is named for, then give it plenty of garden space and leave it to its own devises.

Cotoneaster: In severe climate areas, cut away all winterkilled branches and stems and reshape. Some species of this shrub can get out of hand, so it is important to pay attention to garden location when planting invasive types. Cotoneaster responds well to shearing for a formal look, but also looks wonderful when allowed to meander and arch according to its natural growth habit.

Daphne: Most species do not respond well to heavy pruning, but always remove dead wood in the dormant season. In garden regions that experience heavy snowfall, it is prudent to place a protective frame over older shrubs. Their aging branches are prone to breakage under heavy snows.

Hamamelis (witch hazel): Very little pruning is necessary except for the removal of dead branches in the dormant season. However, some of the larger species lose their vigor as they age and benefit immensely from the removal of a few of their oldest branches.

Paeonia suffruiticosa (**tree peony**): These showy tree-like shrubs need little care, except for basic maintenance pruning for woody perennials.

Physocarpus opulifolius (**ninebark**): Some of these species grow very tall and may lose flowering on their lateral branches as these branches die back. This shrub can be rejuvenated by cutting close to the ground in the dormant season every three years or so.

Potentilla: Renew potentilla shrubs by removing one third of the oldest canes or by cutting the entire plant back in the dormant season.

Rosa (rose): It is beneficial to remove some of the oldest canes right down to the ground after the first bloom period. All other canes should be cut back to 12 to 18 inches in the dormant period depending upon your climate. Try to cut each cane back to an outfacing bud. Dead wood should be cut out on an on-going basis. Hybrid tea roses should be left with three to five strong canes following pruning. Shrub roses can be left taller and pruned only to maintain health and control size.

Sambucus (elder): To maintain foliage color, cut back all stems to within six to eight inches of the crown during the dormant season. As an alternative, prune out old wood and cut all other stems half way back on a regular basis in late winter.

Stewartia: This tree-like shrub needs very little pruning except for the removal of dead, diseased or crossed wood.

WOODY PLANTS AND SHRUBS
THAT DEFY THE RULES

Berberis (barberry): These shrubs can be pruned into formal shapes or left to ramble. To keep a formal shape year round, clip two or three times throughout the growing season. Older shrub forms can be severely cut back in the dormant season for rejuvenation.

Calluna and Erica (heather and heath): Heather blooms in late summer or fall, while heath blooms in the spring. Trim heather plants in the dormant season to stimulate dense new growth and to promote summer flowering. Prune heath right after the flowering period ends in the spring to keep plants from becoming straggly and to rejuvenate. Unless you have *Erica arborea* or *E. vegans,* try to avoid cutting into old wood.

Hydrangea: This group of shrubs does not easily fit into any pruning category. There are approximately 40 species and 500 cultivars of hydrangeas and since some shrubs flower on old wood and others on new wood, it is essential to know which plants you have in order to prune properly. Since this is a beloved garden shrub and often causes confusion to gardeners, I have decided to list a few of the most common species or cultivars and place them in categories according to their individual pruning requirements.

Many hydrangeas need very little pruning, but some of them can get quite large and should be cut back each season to keep their shape and confine them to their garden space. All dead wood should be removed each year and older shrubs can be rejuvenated by cutting one third of the older stems to the ground during their proper pruning season. This restorative work may reduce some flowering during the summer season, but it will greatly enhance the health of the shrub. Hydrangeas can be deadheaded anytime during the growing season as long as only the spent blossoms at the branch tips are removed so as not to disturb developing buds below. Always keep your cuts above the first set of strong leaves, so no harm will be done to early forming flower buds on hydrangeas in category one.

Category One

H. macrophylla (all big leaf hydrangeas) and *H. quercifolia* (oak-leaf).

This group of hydrangeas blooms on new shoots off of old wood which have had 9 to 10 months to grow before bloom time. As soon as the flowers begin to fade, but no later than August 1st, prune these shrubs back to control size and shape. Throughout June and July, long-stemmed flowering branches can be cut for floral arrangements, because next year's flower buds will have not set yet.

Category Two

H. paniculata ('Grandiflora', 'Tardiva' and 'Pink Diamond') and *H. arborescens* 'Annabelle'.

These hydrangeas bloom on current season's growth and can be cut back hard in the dormant season. They grow prolifically in summer and put on a great show. The cultivar, 'Annabelle', can be cut back all the way to the ground in the fall to tidy it up, since it can create an unsightly mess going into winter. In milder regions, try cutting 'Annabelle' back to 12–18 inches above ground. This will encourage a stronger woody framework which should do a better job of supporting the large, droopy flower heads.

Spirea: While most spireas flower in the spring on wood grown the previous season, a few flower in the summer on new wood. It is important to know your plants so you can prune the summer flowering shrubs in the dormant season and the others right after flowering in the spring. Both types can be thinned on a regular basis to maintain vigorous growth and profuse flowering.

PRUNING VINES

Actinidia kolomikta (**kiwi**): Ornamental kiwi vines need regular pruning to keep them from forming dense, unruly masses. Prune them by heading or thinning on a regular basis to allow light and air to reach their interiors.

Akebia quinata (**five-leaf akebia**): This charming vine tends to curl around onto itself as it grows and therefore needs regular tying up or cutting back to avoid a tangled mess. After they bloom in the spring, they can be cut way back to rejuvenate them or to tidy them up.

Aristolochia durior (**Dutchman's pipe**): Prune these vigorous vines back hard in the dormant season to keep them within their designated space. To expose their flowers, some of their large leaves can be selectively removed when they are in flower.

Clematis: This group of plants can cause much vexation and hair pulling to inexperienced gardeners. This is because there are over 1,000 different types of clematis, if you count all the species, wild varieties and cultivars around the world, many of which have quite different growth habits and flowering times. And to further complicate things, some clematis flower on old wood, others on new wood, while the remaining ones flower on both old and new wood.

Species clematis are the most straightforward in their pruning needs while many of the cultivars can be tricky to figure out. *The key is to know which clematis plants you have in your garden, and when each of them blooms, in order to know how and when to prune them.*

Most reference books on pruning divide clematis into three distinct pruning categories. If you can't figure out which pruning method to use, delve into the excellent reference books for pruning clematis listed in the back of this book. Meanwhile, the following rules of thumb should provide the basics to successfully prune most clematis plants.

Clematis plants that bloom only in the spring need very little pruning. This group all flower from the nodes of the previous year's shoots. Pruning is not really necessary except when they have outgrown their allotted space. *If you wish to revitalize them or contain them, cut them back right after they finish flowering so as to not remove next year's flowers.*

Clematis which flower on the current season's growth after early summer are considered to be mid- to late- summer flowering clematis. These plants should be pruned back in the dormant season to the first set of strong buds or nodes. This severe pruning stimulates strong, new growth and promotes more prolific flowering.

Clematis that bloom twice a season (on new wood and old wood) do not require major pruning except for removing dead or weak stems as the dormant season ends in the spring. If you wish to do some selective pruning, do it immediately after the first round of flowers in the spring working downwards from the top of the plant. I compromise by cutting my *Clematis tangutica* back by one-third at the end of the dormant season before the first round of flowers. I lose some of the early flowers but this chopping back rejuvenates the entire plant for the more spectacular show of late summer blossoms and seed heads.

Some clematis plants behave like other herbaceous perennials in that their above-ground parts die back to ground level as the growing season comes to an end. In this case, remove all the dead stems and foliage once a plant has completely died back.

Euonymus: The shrub forms can be clipped for a more formal look. Creeping euonymus needs to be cut back on a regular basis or it will invade neighboring garden space.

Hedera helix (**English ivy**), *Parthenocissus quinquefolia* (**Virginia creeper**) and *Parthenocissus tricuspidata* (**Boston ivy**): Each of these vines needs regular maintenance to contain their spread, or they can take over parts of a house they weren't meant to cover or completely smother whatever lies in their path. They can all be cut back hard in the dormant season and always remove damaged sections on a regular basis because they lose the ability to reattach.

Hydrangea anomala **subsp.** *petiolaris* (**climbing hydrangea**): Prune these climbers in late dormant season to control growth and to stimulate new wood.

Lonicera x *heckrottii* (**ever-blooming honeysuckle**): These vigorous vines should be headed back and/or thinned out of all excess stems during the dormant season each year. Always remove suckers on a regular basis.

Polygonum aubertii (silver lace vine): Prune this vine late in the dormant season to avoid frost damage in colder areas. This vine is a vigorous grower during the growing season, and it blooms more profusely if cut back to one or two stems each year.

Vitis (grape): To use as an arbor cover or other decorative landscape feature, allow this wonderful vine to ramble on its own and prune it only to keep it within its designated garden space. Of course, cut out all dead or diseased wood and thin or head back to promote better light and air circulation.

Wisteria floribunda (Japanese wisteria), *Wisteria sinensis* (Chinese wisteria) and *Wisteria macrostachya* (Kentucky wisteria): This prolific-growing vine needs pruning several times a year to keep it in check and to promote better flowering. It is a good idea to train it from a young age and allow just a few of the stronger branches to grow lengthwise. In the dormant season, all the side branches on the main leaders should be cut back to two or three buds. The short branches bearing these remaining buds are called spurs and it is these buds which produce the blossoms. During the growing season, it is important to remove all the leafless shoots (suckers), which sprout prolifically as a result of the severe pruning carried out earlier in the dormant season. Wisteria is a frustrating vine to grow in colder regions of the world. Many gardeners choose to grow this vine because of its magnificent flowers and therefore can be quite disappointed when their vines refuse to flower. Many wisteria vines take years of maturing before they finally flower and often fail to flower following an exceptionally severe winter. So, always buy the hardiest plants for your climate and religiously prune them every year; these are two aspects of growing wisteria that are in your control. Otherwise, it may help to send a few prayers to the flower gods.

The Dirt on "Dirt"

MARCH

Soil Composition, Testing and Amending

s the snow begins to melt and patches of earth slowly reveal themselves, my hands itch to dig in the dirt again. After months indoors, I can hardy wait to begin clearing our gardens for the new growing season. As I work at these tasks, signs of emerging plant life are everywhere. Plump buds are perched to unfurl their secrets, crocuses, snowdrops and hellebores bejewel the woodland garden, and early herbaceous plants are peeking out of the warming soil. Each spring, as I greet these awakening friends, I marvel at the regenerative powers of the natural world. Thank goodness humans can only be reborn ritualistically!

This first month of spring at Muddy Creek is the ideal time to clear away leftover perennial debris and expose the soil for inspection. As I do my spring cleanup chores, I rake leaves and debris carefully to avoid breaking tender, fledgling plant tips. I postpone digging or any removal of weeds until the ground has totally thawed and dried out — usually in April, depending upon the severity of the winter. However, this timetable can vary considerably in other hardiness zones. Therefore, I am putting off discussions concerning weeding and planting until April and May. For the month of March, I would like to focus entirely on soil.

Every gardener has unique compositions of soil inherited as the earth evolved through the ages, blessing or cursing them with specific types of soil. A rare few have been given "perfect" soil, while the rest of us spend most of our garden lives amending and enriching what nature has randomly bestowed upon us. These March discussions explain what constitutes good garden soil, how to determine what type of soil you have in your perennial gardens, and how to amend soils in order to grow vigorous, healthy plants year in and year out.

Good soil is a gardener's staff of life. Within its depths lie the essential nutrients to satisfy most plants. The best soils are comprised of sand, silt, clay and decomposed organic matter (humus) in balanced proportions. Air and water bind these four ingredients together to form soft, malleable crumbs. Good soil should be sandy enough to drain well, but contain enough clay and organic matter to hold onto its nutrients. Many gardeners live in relentless pursuit of the ideal soil (myself included).

SAND AND CLAY:
SOIL'S TWO MAIN INGREDIENTS

Sand is comprised of minute particles of rock debris surrounded by air pockets. Water flows freely through sand, and as a consequence, sandy soils have excellent drainage capabilities. Roots can easily push their way through sand, and air is always in plentiful supply.

However, a major drawback to soils high in sand is that they lack fertility. Water rushes through so fast that valuable nutrients are constantly being leached away. In extremely sandy soils, perennials have a tough time surviving because most of the available water drains to a lower water table than their roots can reach. (Desert plants have learned to survive by adapting their roots and modified leaves to act as reservoirs.)

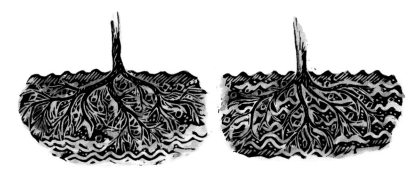

Clay soils lie at the opposite end of the scale. Clay consists of fine, mineral particles, each encased by a thin, water-grabbing film which causes these particles to coagulate and hold water. As a result, clay soil is heavy, airless and difficult to work with. Water tends to pool on its surface, and when it finally seeps into the soil, it tends to collect in planting holes where it either rots or drowns roots. Muddy Creek has heavy clay soils (So heavy that I have made earthenware pots from it), and many a plant died before I realized that water was collecting in the bottom of

my carefully amended holes. I was unwittingly creating underground reservoirs directly beneath each plant. Needless to say, I quickly learned to amend an entire bed at one time to encourage water to disperse evenly throughout the bed.

Clay's main attribute is that it is rich in nutrients which are not easily leached away. Since water has a difficult time penetrating clay soils, these soils are able to hold onto their food reserves. (After years of adding compost to our clay soils, we now have some of the richest soil in Addison County.)

Soil Formation and Composition

Soil types are partly determined by the types of rock (parent material) that were worn away to create them. Most soils are created from rock that has weathered in place (local soils). These local soils tend to be a combination of particles of all sizes from silt to stone and are more balanced than transported soils. Transported soils are soils that have been relocated, usually by glacier action, rain and wind. These soils are sifted and sorted as they travel, dumping rocks in river beds and depositing silt in low-lying regions at the end of their journey.

Variation in soils also depends upon how much organic matter is present and the amount of surface area of the mineral particles. *Perfect soils are composed of about two-thirds rock particles, from small stones to clay. The other third consists of decayed animal and vegetable matter (with its substantial populations of living organisms), ample water and copious amounts of air.*

Soil is capable of holding water in two ways: First, by its decomposing organic matter which acts like a sponge, and by the thin film which coats each clay particle.

Soil Chemistry and Testing

It is easy to conduct a simple percolation ("perc") test to determine the drainage capacity of your garden soil. Dig several holes 12 inches wide and 12 inches deep in various areas of your perennial gardens. Cover the holes with plastic for a few days to let the soil dry out.

Remove the plastic, fill each hole to the top with water and record the amount of time it takes for each hole to drain. If all the holes are completely empty after 10 to 30 minutes, your soil is fine and count your blessings.

> The capacity of soil to store water is one of
> a gardener's primary concerns.

If a hole drains too quickly (in less than 10 minutes), then that section of the garden would benefit from additions of compost to help the soil retain moisture. If a hole still contains water after 30 minutes to four hours, your soil has a high content of clay. The best remedy is to add copious amounts of compost which will introduce air and lighten the structure of your soil.

Most soils do quite well supporting perennial plant life without amending the pH or using fertilizers, as long as balanced compost is added on a regular basis. A compost heap acts like a gardener's own cow, converting waste materials into a form that can be easily absorbed by the soil. It is almost impossible to add too much organic matter, except in the case of extra fluffy, acid soils which already contain high levels of humus. (Pine forests, with their thick carpets of needles, have this type of soil.)

A complete soil analysis will tell you what your soil does or does not need. To have your soil tested, check with your local extension service or buy a self-testing kit from a garden store. Soil tests determine soil type, pH, organic matter content and available phosphate and potash. Consult the chart for the minimum standards your soil should meet.

> *Minimum Standards for Perennial Garden Soils from the Perennial Plant Association*
>
> pH of 5.5 to 6.5
> Organic matter — 5% by weight
> 50 lbs. per acre of phosphate (P)
> 120 lbs. per acre of potassium (K)

MINERAL NUTRIENTS AND PH VALUES REQUIRED BY PERENNIAL PLANTS

The three life-sustaining elements — carbon, hydrogen and oxygen — are provided to plants by air and water. Soil provides the six other main elements essential for growing healthy perennial plants: nitrogen, phosphorus, potassium, calcium, magnesium and sulfur. Trace elements, which include iron, manganese, boron, copper, zinc and molybdenum, are only required in small amounts. In most cases, it is just the first three of the main soil elements — nitrogen, phosphorus and potassium — that need regular topping off, and that usually only occurs when growing vegetable or fruit crops that take more from the soil than is being returned. If you regularly add compost to your gardens, the essential elements should be present in sufficient amounts.

ORGANIC SOIL AMENDMENTS

Amending with compost is the best way to incorporate organic matter into perennial beds. A well-balanced compost contains a wide variety of organic waste materials such as leaves, manure, grass clippings, hay or straw, bark, sawdust, sphagnum peat moss, food remains and bio-waste, to name just a few.

Compost and rotted manures are both complete foods for the soil because they feed its structure as well as its chemistry. However, a couple of cautions are in order. Fresh manure should never be spread directly on perennial beds without first going though an aging period. Manure is so rich in nitrogen that it can kill or injure plants. The best way to use manure is to layer it into your compost pile as one of the main nitrogen-rich ingredients. (See the September chapter for complete discussions on this topic.)

Poor soil is usually at the root of 80% of all plant problems.

It is also important to know that even though manure contains all the essential nutrients, it has a low ratio of nutrients relative to its bulk. A ton of manure contains only 30 pounds of the essential nutrients. This is another reason it works best to mix manure into your compost pile where it can join forces with a wide variety of other ingredients. Many manures contain copious amounts of weed seeds. Horse manure is the biggest carrier, cow manure is second and chicken manure contains the fewest weed seeds. These seeds are killed when manure is used as one of the ingredients in building a fresh pile of compost. (The army of decomposing agents in a compost pile cause the pile to "cook" (heat up to 160°F).

BENEFITS OF ADDING ORGANIC MATTER
TO PERENNIAL BEDS

Soil structure is one of the most important factors in growing perennials. As soils become deficient in organic matter, they lose their structure, becoming compressed and lifeless. When organic matter is added to sandy soils, the soil becomes more capable of retaining water and nutrients. Organic matter added to clay lightens its structure by creating more air spaces. Roots need air almost as much as they need water. With the exception of water and bog plants, roots die if waterlogged for long periods. I can't emphasize enough the importance of providing deep, well-drained and well-aerated soil for your perennial gardens. The deeper plants can grow their roots, the safer they will be during periods of droughts and floods.

Organic matter's other primary job is to provide a continuous supply of food. As soil organisms feed on organic matter, they cause it to decay and release its nutrients. There is seldom any need to add other fertilizers to your gardens if you religiously feed your soil with organic matter. Mature compost is by far the most effective way to add organic matter. The constant stream of slow-release nutrients provided by a balanced compost can actually boost plant growth by 20 to 100%.

High levels of organic matter in soil also reduces erosion, keeps the pH buffered toward neutral (neither too acidic nor too alkaline) and even protects against toxic substances. Soils rich in organic matter are alive with beneficial microbes and earthworms, which help keep disease-carrying microbes in check.

CHOOSING THE BEST COMPOST
FOR PERENNIAL GARDENS

Which type of compost to use depends upon its cost, availability in your area, and the particular needs of your soil. Composts range all the way from homemade concoctions to a wide selection of commercial products. (For details on how to make balanced compost, see the pages for September.) As a result, composts differ significantly in composition. If the raw materials are not mixed in the proper ratios, there can be serious nutrient imbalances. For example, composts made from too high a percentage of woody, stalky materials which contain high levels of carbon tend to be deficient in nitrogen. Conversely, composts made mainly from green materials, such as grass clippings, manure or foodstuff, contain high levels of nitrogen but lack the structure provided by carbon.

At the present time, no national standard seems to exist for rating the quality of commercially produced compost. However, most garden centers sell excellent compost acquired from local companies with good reputations.

When purchasing compost, look for some basic characteristics. *Mature compost should have a wholesome, "earthy" smell and should be broken down enough that it is difficult to recognize any of its raw materials. It should be soft and crumbly when held in your hand.* Compost that hasn't been allowed to mature enough robs soil of nitrogen as the microbes complete the decomposition process.

Finally, try to buy compost that's neither too wet nor too dry. In the first case, you're paying extra money to haul water, and in the second case, it's dusty to handle and less abundant in beneficial organisms.

WHEN AND HOW TO ADD AMENDMENTS TO SOIL

Late spring and fall are the two best times to amend soils. Microorganisms depend upon the warmth and moisture in the soil at those times of the year to break down organic matter into humus. Microbes in general are not active in soil that is too cold, too wet or too acidic.

Amending the soil in spring is especially beneficial because plants are in need of extra nutrients as they expend their energies putting forth new growth. Also, soil tends to get compressed after the hard conditions of winter and it benefits immensely from additions of compost each spring.

In fall, a few inches of new compost laid on the surface provides a protective winter mulch. Any compost that remains in the spring can be worked into the soil. This twice-yearly program of soil amending supplies a steady stream of nutrients and also bolsters soil structure on a continuous basis.

For existing beds, be sure to use mature compost (almost completely decomposed). Otherwise, as said earlier, it may rob nutrients from the soil and starve

plants as it breaks down further. In spring, work 2 to 4 inches of compost into perennial beds in which the soil is 8 to 12 inches deep. To ensure ample feeding and soil conditioning, make sure you work the compost as deeply into the soil as possible. It will break down more slowly and more efficiently than if just spread on top of the soil. However, be careful not to damage roots, especially plants like rhododendrons and azaleas whose roots are very close to the surface.

When establishing new beds, it is even more important to work compost into the soil as deeply and evenly as possible. It is also a good idea to add extra phosphorus at this time because new plants require more phosphorus while they are establishing their root systems. It is a good idea to allow new beds to sit for a few months before planting. This allows the compost to release some of its nutrients as it continues to decay and for the soil to mature structurally. Gardeners often prepare new beds in this manner in late summer or early fall for planting the following spring.

To grow healthy plants year in and year out,
garden soils should be amended regularly with
organic matter (compost). Organic matter
reintroduces structure to depleted or compressed
soils, allows air and water to flow more freely,
and feeds the soil by slowly releasing its
nutrients as it continues to decompose.

Any weed left unturned will surely
come back to haunt you.

APRIL

Weeding, Edging,
Fertilizers and Herbicides

verywhere in the garden, plants are springing to life eager to flaunt their beauty. Daffodils and violets have poked up their heads in the vinca bank, creating an impressionistic painting more pleasing to my eye than any rendered on canvas. My joy in this beauty is unbounded. This is the time of the year I most frequently thank the gods for allowing me to be the caretaker of this of little bit of earth.

Weeding is a top priority this month, allowing the reptilian side of my nature to enjoy a brief period of dominance. My style of weeding involves creeping and crawling on hands and knees amongst my beds with trowel and claw tool in constant motion. Any friend dropping by unexpectedly would be appalled to witness my earth-covered body slithering along in complete abandonment. But these are actually some of my happiest garden hours. As my face comes to within inches of each plant, a myriad of earthy smells act as a tonic to my soul. Also, as I am up close and personal with each plant, it is almost impossible for any weed to escape my merciless eye.

Besides weeding, there are other important garden chores in April, such as edging garden beds, feeding the soil and taking care of any specific plant requirements with special food or soil additives. These April pages focus mainly on the techniques and merits of proper weeding, edging and amending, but they also include short discussions on chemical fertilizers and herbicides. Try to avoid neglecting these April chores or you may spend the rest of the summer playing catch up. The old adage, "Never put off until later what you can do right now," is so perfectly apt in April.

Weeds need lots of light and room to grow in order to thrive. In spring, before garden plants have leafed out and shaded the bare spaces, weeds have a huge advantage. Procrastinating at this critical time of year allows weeds to get firmly entrenched, making them more difficult to remove later. *As soon as you can dig a handful of soil that holds its form for a few seconds but then falls apart into soft crumbs, you can safely begin weeding.*

> A good rule of thumb is to remove perennial and biennial weeds as soon as you spot them and pull annual weeds before they flower to prevent them from seeding in.

WEEDING TECHNIQUES

Work from the edges of beds toward the center in three-to-four-foot swaths, paying special attention to weeds near the base of perennials. Pulling these weeds is a top priority because they compete with plants for light and nutrients. Use a kneeling pad or board to disperse your weight evenly to avoid unnecessary compression of the soil (or of your back). Compressed soil makes it more difficult for plants to receive optimal amounts of air, water and nutrients.

Loosen soil with a trowel or spade fork depending upon the size of the weeds. Work slowly and carefully in densely planted areas. The roots of most perennial plants lie no more than six to eight inches deep, which makes it easy to damage them. Remove each weed by grasping it as far down the root system as possible and then slowly tease it out. If you miss any of the roots on the first pull, try to dig out any substantial parts left behind. I have often chased chopped-off grass roots several feet knowing how capable they are of re-sprouting.

Dig out an entire plant if weeds have become thoroughly enmeshed in its root system. Carefully loosen the root ball with your hands to extricate any remaining weeds. Always replant immediately and water thoroughly to prevent the roots from drying out. At this time of year, plants are very resistant to potential damage from this process and should not be adversely affected by this procedure.

For large clumps of plants such as lamb's ears, start in the middle of the plant clump and slice straight down with a spade shovel. Cut the plant into square sec-

tions, remove each section and gently tease out the weed roots with your hands. This method is far more efficient than continually picking at the enmeshed weeds throughout the season.

The simple practice of mowing lawns eliminates weeds. Weeds run out of stored energy in their root systems if they are unable to grow mature leaves. When mowed regularly, the weeds remain too small to survive, while grasses thrive since they are no longer in competition with the weeds.

CATEGORIES OF WEEDS

Weeds even a novice can recognize

These weeds are the easiest to contend with since most gardeners can recognize them. Common weeds vary greatly between garden zones or even within the same zone. Weeds I constantly do battle with include burdock, red and white clover, chicory, common mullein, dandelion, ragweed, stinging nettles, yellow sorrel, and thistles. Terry and I love living in rural Vermont surrounded by farmland, but it does have a few downsides. Bird's foot trefoil and cow vetch, which were originally introduced as forage for cattle, have become the bane of my gardening existence. They invade garden beds and try their best to take over every available inch of bare soil. Each year, I pack garden voids with new plants to deter these tenacious weeds from gaining a foothold.

Try to get rid of your common weeds by the method most appropriate for their individual root systems. Dandelion and burdock both have long tap-roots and should be lifted out using a spade fork, since they are capable of growing back from any root part left behind. Newly sprouted vetch pulls out fairly easily while bird's foot trefoil seems to have roots of iron.

Each spring be sure to pull out invading weeds before they flower and set seed. A large number of an-

Identifying and knowing your enemy is half the battle.

nuals self-sow in gardens each year. You will want to remove or transplant any seedlings which don't fit into your garden design. I happen to love the way the annuals, *Euphorbia marginata* and datura (angel's trumpet), randomly seed into the perennial beds, accentuating the naturalistic style of our gardens.

Hard-to-identify invaders

Keep an eye on mystery plants in order to identify them as soon as possible. There is little to be gained from nurturing this type of plant any longer than necessary. They compete with surrounding plants for nutrients, light and moisture and take up valuable garden space.

When I add new herbaceous plants late in the season, I leave these plants with eight inch stalks and often place identification markers next to them during fall clean-up. This prevents me from mistakenly removing them during spring weeding.

Garden plants which tend to overrun their space

If your garden contains some of these invasive-type plants, now is the time to deal with them. Lamb's ears and several species of euphorbia are good examples of perennials which behave like weeds if left to their own devices. Lamb's ears needs to be divided on a regular basis to keep it contained and many euphorbia seed prolifically into every inch of open soil. Plants such as aegopodium (bishop's weed) and purple loosestrife are highly invasive and should be on every gardener's bad-plant list.

EDGING PERENNIAL BEDS

Most gardens benefit from a cut edge at the front of perennial beds. Nothing makes a garden look better than a mown lawn at its feet. Also, a cut edge is an attractive garden feature unto itself, and is less costly and more natural looking than plastic or metal edging.

Well-cut edges are perfect deterrents to weeds. Also, it is easy to spot weeds along the edge because beds are usually bordered by lawn, ground covers, shrubs or other plant material easily distinguishable from weeds. In the spring, if you first cut and define edges, you gain a jump-start on weeding the interiors of beds.

To cut an edge, use a spade shovel and insert it into the ground to its depth. Force the handle toward the ground to loosen the soil and to slice through any protruding roots. You can follow up with a spade fork to tease out any remaining roots that the shovel may have missed or severed. I find half-moon edgers to be not quite as effective because they don't penetrate as deeply or loosen the soil as well.

Edging trenches should be straight up and down on the lawn side of the cliff and gradually sloping on the bedside. Be sure to take the time to make the trench as deep as the roots of the adjoining lawn or ground covers. Roots can't grow in open air and will dry up and die if they try to bridge the trench.

Next spring, I plan to borrow my friend Robin's power-driven edger and it will probably spoil me for life. I'm sure I'll be dropping hints to Terry for a rather expensive Christmas gift.

The fertilizer industry works on
the premise that you need to feed plants;
in contrast, organic gardeners feed the soil,
so that it can feed plants.

SUPPLEMENTING GARDENS WITH FERTILIZERS

Let plants and soil tell you their needs. New beds, or existing beds which began with little organic matter, take awhile to build up their organic content. The observant gardener notices when a particular plant or an entire group of plants is not growing well.

Soils deficient in nitrogen and/or phosphorus can cause stunted plant growth. Chlorosis, exhibited by a plant's leaves turning pale green or yellow, usually indicates that a plant is suffering from a lack of a specific nutrient, such as nitrogen, iron or magnesium. Or, if you are unable to easily dig in a certain area of the garden and the earthworm population seems low, the soil is begging you to work in a few inches of a well-decayed compost as soon as possible.

If you are planning to add a layer of un-decomposed mulch, such as roughly shredded bark, as a protective summer mulch, it might be smart to add an organic fertilizer at the same time. Soil microbes rob the soil of nitrogen as they break down and digest bark mulch during the growing season.

> Specific minerals and nutrients are essential building blocks of plant growth. If your soil has insufficient quantities of any of them, it may be necessary to add extra fertilizers to the garden above and beyond the addition of compost.

CHOOSING THE BEST FERTILIZER FOR YOUR GARDEN'S DEFICIENCIES

Most of the time it is safest to use organic or chemical fertilizers containing all three of the main plant nutrients: nitrogen, phosphorus and potassium. Experienced gardeners can successfully add individual nutrients in the proper amounts, but unless you're one of them, it is advisable to use a complete, balanced fertilizer. This helps prevent overfeeding plants with too heavy a concentration of any specific nutrient. For example, adding too much quick-release nitrogen can promote too much leaf growth and not enough flowering. An excess of phosphate can cause an excessive buildup of salts, which can burn roots and kill plants.

If soil tests (discussed in March) show deficiencies, a fertilizer containing nutrients in the proper ratio should be added using the recommended application rates listed on the product. Pro-Grow 5-3-4 is just one of many balanced, all-natural fertilizers on the market and is produced by North Country Organics in Bradford, Vermont. Organic fertilizers combine a wide variety of natural ingredients such as ground-up or dried remains of animal life (fish meal, seaweed, dried blood and bonemeal are some of the most common) to produce a complete, all natural plant food.

Chemical fertilizers are exactly the opposite because they are produced by artificially combining chemical elements. Garden centers carry a wide variety of products, in both liquid and granular forms. Inorganic fertilizers supply the same nutrients as organic products, but there is a higher risk of harming plants if over applied. Chemical products react directly on plants, are costly to purchase, and do not remain in the soil very long (unlike compost or organic fertilizers which slowly release their nutrients into the soil).

The ratio numbers on fertilizer products denote the percentage by weight of nitrogen, phosphorus and potassium, the three most important nutrients for feeding perennials. A 5-3-4 fertilizer consists of 5% nitrogen, 3% phosphorus and 4% potassium along with small amounts of the other less vital nutrients. This is a good all-purpose mix for supplementing most perennial beds.

Lawns respond well to a fertilizer rich in nitrogen, such as 10-6-4, while bulbs are best fed with a phosphorus rich fertilizer such as 4-12-8. Acid-loving plants, such as heathers and rhododendrons, benefit from an addition of sulfur if the soil is too alkaline, while lime can be worked into acid soil to sweeten the

Decomposing organic matter, such as compost, slowly releases an undetermined amount of natural nutrients into the soil; while chemical fertilizers immediately supply plants with specific amounts of chosen nutrients.

soil for alkaline-loving plants such as iris. However, the majority of perennial plants survive quite well in most garden soils except in the case of severe acidic or alkaline conditions.

ORGANIC VERSUS CHEMICAL WEED CONTROL

The best way to serve the natural world is to use organic compost and mulch on your garden beds rather than rely on chemicals to kill weeds. Most chemical weed killers effect the microorganisms in the soil and surrounding air in the same way that chemotherapy kills good cells along with bad cells in the human body. Also, there is evidence that pre-emergent weed killers build up in the soil, in which case they have long term effects on the health of your ecosystem.

The only weed killer I feel comfortable using is a systemic weed control such as glyphosate, more commonly known as Roundup®. This type of product is safest and most effective when applied in the spring, just as weeds are emerging. The poison travels throughout a weed's vascular system, which results in the death of the entire plant. Glyphosate is one of the few chemical herbicides that has little or no affect on the surrounding soil if used properly. The best method of application is to paint young leaves with a brush. But a sprayer can be used if you direct the spray directly toward the weeds and there is no wind.

Ecologically, it is much more desirable to completely redo a bed that has been taken over by weeds than to attempt to eradicate the weeds with a chemical killer. First, remove all small perennials from the bed and put them in a safe holding spot. Then till the old soil thoroughly to loosen the entrenched weeds.

> The more natural the approach, the less chance
> of affecting the balance of nature.

Carefully replant all your plants, making sure their roots are completely free of weeds. Finish by placing several layers of wet newspapers over the soil topped off with two-to-four inches of compost. This top dressing of papers and compost will kill the remaining weeds and improve the structure and fertility of the soil. This process is best done in the fall in order to allow the paper time to decompose over the dormant winter months. In the spring you will have the pleasure of a weed-free, soil-amended bed.

On terraces and pathways, where it is difficult to get at the roots of weeds, burning weeds with a propane torch is an effective, environmentally sound tool for eliminating weeds. Torches are inexpensive, simple to use and leave an ash residue which is beneficial to the soil.

Gardeners are incessantly moving plants from one
place to another, while a plant's nature is to stay put.

MAY

Planting, Dividing, Mulching, and Staking

ay is an exhilarating month at Muddy Creek. The time has come to reap some well-earned rewards following months of prep chores. The plant nurseries are opening, and once again I can attempt to satiate my incurable lust for new plants. My car seems to have a mind of its own as it inevitably swerves into any garden center I happen to drive by. Once I'm on the premises, my biggest challenge is to stem my urges to adopt each and every plant that I don't already own. I often commandeer the smallest cart available, knowing that my addiction to new plants is the same as a bear's for wild berries.

During the growing season, I spend many hours wandering my gardens with pad and pencil in hand, scheming of ways to make room for new "must have" plants. Sometimes I actually remember to take these notes with me on my buying trips. It is so easy to get sidetracked when surrounded by hundreds of seductive perennials. I have also discovered that it is wise to purchase only as many plants as I can put into the ground within a week. Otherwise, I end up feeling that I've inadvertently entered the nursery business.

Depending on the age and conditions of your gardens, you may need to spend time dividing and transplanting existing perennials before planting newly acquired plants. These May pages present and explain the basic principles, techniques, and "tricks of the trade" to properly carry-out these chores. The chapter ends with a short discussion of mulching, watering and staking after planting.

Happy digging!

Roots are plants' most important organs, but they are often neglected since they spend their lives underground. To quote an anonymous seventeenth century writer, "Those that plant should make their ground fit (for rose trees) before they plant them, and not bury them in a hole like a dead dog." When it comes to planting, there was never a more relevant truism.

THE BEST TIMES TO PLANT AND TRANSPLANT

Depending upon your hardiness zone, April and May are two of the best months to plant. Plants divided or planted in the spring, when the soil is warming, are more quickly stimulated to put down their all-important root systems as they enter the active growing season.

Plants are quite forgiving in early spring. They can be dug, chopped and replanted with hardly a break in their growth. However, the later you plant in the growing season, the more difficult it is for plants to establish themselves. Stress caused by the high heat and lower rainfall in summertime can slow plant growth or even bring it to a halt.

> Rule: Divide spring and summer-blooming perennials
> in late summer and early fall, but wait until spring to
> divide fall-blooming perennials.

Fall is also an excellent time to plant if winter temperatures are not too severe and your hardiness zone is free of early freeze-thaw cycles. At this time of year, root growth is not in competition with new, above-ground growth as it is in the springtime. As stems and foliage slowly die back, roots continue to grow as long as temperatures remain above 45°F.

However, make sure new plants have time to become firmly rooted before the arrival of the first hard frost by planting six weeks prior to that projected date. Large trees and shrubs are an exception to this rule. It is the smaller perennial plants that are endangered if planted too late in the fall. Be sure to provide plenty of water if weather conditions have been on the dry side.

REASONS FOR DIVIDING PERENNIAL PLANTS

Most plants naturally grow larger each year by increasing their mass. They do this in a number of different ways depending upon their species. Perennials that grow from bulbs proliferate by producing offsets (baby bulbs); rhizome-rooted plants such as iris grow more rhizomes; lilac shrubs send up new shoots around the parent shrub; and the highly invasive plant, petasites, madly produces underground runners which pop up all over the place, sometimes yards away from the main plant.

A plant assumes the age of its most recent division.

Vigorous growers, if not held in check, crowd out neighboring plants and begin to compete for light, air, moisture and nutrients. While some continue to remain healthy, others may suffer and even die if left unattended.

Artemisia , daylilies, and iris are a few examples of perennials whose growth patterns cause them to spread out of their allotted garden space. Regular digging and dividing overachieving plants reinvigorates them, and at the same time prevents them from taking over the garden.

Certain types of perennials are subject to die-out in their centers after they reach maturity. Coral bells grow well for four years or more before their centers die; while lamb's ears and veronica exhibit this problem in half that time. Plants which contain dead or damaged parts are more prone to attack by disease and undesirable bugs of all types. Be proactive in dividing these types of plants in order to avoid health problems and to keep control in your garden.

Each year as I divide and transplant, I create a number of new plants from each original plant. This type of plant propagation (vegetative) is the easiest and quickest to perform and has the immediate reward of producing new plants identical to the original ones. I save a substantial amount of money by filling empty spaces in the garden with newly divided plants.

METHODS FOR DIVIDING
AND MOVING PERENNIALS

Before tackling this process, make a plan! Identify which plants will stay and which will be divided, moved, given away or composted. This will save valuable time and energy, and result in less soil disturbance.

Use a sharp spade shovel to dig deeply around each plant clump and then lift out the entire plant, taking as much soil as possible in order to protect the roots. For large, matt-like plants, such as ornamental grasses, you can cut a plant into sections to avoid damaging the plant and its root system while lifting.

A day or so before dividing plants, give them a thorough soaking to ensure that the roots are well saturated and to make digging easier. If you are dividing in the fall, severely prune plant tops back to six inches above the ground in order to see what you are doing. This cutting back also allows newly divided plants to redirect their energies to root growth.

If a plant's center has died out, use a spade shovel to divide the plant into new, smaller sections. Be sure to remove all the dead, rotten or damaged plant parts, saving just the healthy clumps for replanting. You can replant even the tiniest clump as long as the crown is healthy and there a few undamaged roots below. Use a sharp knife to cut apart any entwined roots that you are unable to tease apart with your fingers.

Plants with woody crowns, such as astilbe, are best divided by cutting through their crowns with a sharp knife. Some plants, like Siberian iris, possess extremely dense crowns, which sometimes makes it necessary to employ a sharp hatchet or meat cleaver to cut them cleanly apart. Certain species of old grasses can become so densely matted that the only way to divide them is with an ax, as if you were splitting a log.

Bear in mind, that even if you think you have kept most of a plant's root system intact during the digging process, a significant amount of root tips and hairs

is always lost. Try to evaluate the amount of lost root mass, and then cut back the plant's top accordingly. This is most applicable when subdividing in the fall, since most plants still have a large amount of foliage. In springtime, this is not usually an issue because newly emerging plants have very little foliage.

If an entire garden section has become overrun, your best option is to dig out the entire group of plants and replant the section with the proper amount of plants for the space.

If at all possible, divide and transplant on cloudy or cool days with little wind. This causes less trauma and shock to newly dug plants and makes it easier for them to recover. If temperatures are high and/or a plant is large and leggy, place a shade tent over it for a few days. (Cut back a leggy plant by one-third to one-half if it doesn't seem to be recovering.)

It is important to conduct all planting chores when the soil is not too wet; otherwise you can damage the soil structure and greatly increase its compaction. Long, narrow boards used as walking planks are great tools for reaching the interior areas of large beds.

Ideally, you should prepare all new holes prior to digging the transplants. If you are replanting in well-tended, airy garden soil, make the hole twice the width of the root ball, and its depth no more than the height of the root ball. Be sure to mix a good amount of compost in with the soil that was removed from the hole when filling back in around the plant. To ensure that the plant's root system stays moist, work quickly but carefully.

Tamp down the soil with your hands or feet, depending upon the size of the transplant. Finish replanting by creating a small crater, with a diameter the size of the root ball, around the crown of the plan. This will ensure that the entire root zone receives its fair share of available water. Water thoroughly to make sure the plant is settled in and to eliminate any air pockets that might have been missed during the tamping process.

PLANTING TECHNIQUES
FOR NURSERY BOUGHT PLANTS

Unless a new plant is well saturated with water, it is a good idea to water it an hour or so before planting. Always give a thorough soaking to any plants that have dried out in their nursery pots.

Depending upon the size of the plant, use a hand spade or shovel to dig a planting hole that is at least two times as wide as the root ball. In heavy, clay soils, you may need to dig the hole twice as deep as the root ball (with the exception of large shrubs and trees to be discussed later). If digging deeper than the root ball, be sure to tamp the newly dug bottom soil firmly to avoid settling later.

Be sure that the crown of the plant sits exactly at ground level. If placed too high in the ground, plants can dry out or even pop out of the ground during the freeze-thaw cycles of wintertime. If placed too low, they become subject to collar rot and other fungal diseases. Certain plants, such as peonies, have overwintering buds that lie fairly near the surface, and if planted too deeply, blossom production can be affected. The simple trick of laying a garden stake across a hole after seating a plant is an easy way of determining if the plant has been placed at the proper depth.

Container Plants

Plants purchased in containers usually slide out of their pots fairly easily. But, sometimes it is necessary to turn a potted plant on its side and press firmly all the way around the pot to loosen the root ball. Keep a hand across the top of the pot to prevent the soil and plant from separating during this process. If roots are growing through the bottom of a pot, making it difficult to slide the plant out, cut off the protruding roots with a sharp knife.

Once a plant has been removed from its pot, check to see if its roots have become enmeshed. If this is the case, hold the root ball in your hand and cut the bottom edge in three places with sharp hand-held pruners. This releases the roots so they can easily branch out once they have been planted. In the case of extremely matted root balls, feel free to cut away a half inch or so across the bottom of the root ball.

Burlap-Wrapped Trees

Trees and shrubs with large root balls are usually held together by burlap, possibly with a cage of wire for extra support. Thoroughly examine a burlap-wrapped plant before purchasing to make sure there are no major breaks in the root ball. If the root ball rocks or moves in sections, the roots may be damaged or dried out. After purchase, keep large, wrapped plants in the shade. Water and mulch them well to protect them from drying out until planting time.

Plant all trees and shrubs in a hole two to three times as wide but no deeper than the height of the root ball. (If large plants are placed on firm soil, there is little chance for them to sink lower once planted.) To help avoid the pitfall of planting too deeply, cut the burlap away from the top of a wrapped plant and remove any excess soil from its crown. This allows a clear view of the uppermost horizontal roots and makes it much easier to position the plant at its proper depth. Also, cut the wire in a number of places, partially open the burlap, and loosen it around the upper half of the plant. Use a sharp knife to cut away any excess burlap, leaving just enough in four spots to grasp and to gently lower the plant into its hole. After placing in the hole, pull and coax the burlap slowly out from under the plant. It is important to avoid breaking apart the root ball as that can seriously damage the plant. It is fine to leave some of the burlap around the underside of the root

ball because roots can grow through burlap as it decays. This is far better than doing serious damage by man-handling the burlap out from under a heavy tree or shrub. However, make certain that the burlap is not made of a synthetic material. If it is synthetic, it must be removed completely because it will take years to break down, if ever, in which case the roots will be trapped and you'll end up with a dead tree.

Most trees and some shrubs need to be supported by stakes in their first year or two to give them stability in their new home. This is especially true for tall thin trees in windy locations. Drive in three stakes evenly spaced around a tree and use strong but flexible wire to brace the tree with the stakes. Small six-inch sections of rubber hose should be used to cover the wires where they come in direct contact with the tree trunk. (I cut up an old garden hose for this purpose.) Make sure that your staking allows a tiny bit of movement so that the tree or shrub can maintain a small amount of flexibility. After a year or two, remove the stakes in late spring to keep plants from becoming too dependent upon their support stakes.

Bareroot Plants

Bareroot plants have several advantages over plants purchased in pots. Since all the soil has been carefully removed from their root systems, they are much easier to transport and handle. As a result, a bareroot plant can be bought at a much lower price than an identical plant sold in a pot. One of the few downsides to bareroot plants is that they can only be shipped when they are dormant, so there is just a small window of time in the spring when you can purchase and plant them. Depending upon your area's hardiness zone, late April or May is the optimal time to plant bareroot plants. The warm soil and frequent rainfall in spring provide the perfect conditions to jump-start them out of their dormant state and into a period of fast growth.

Always check to make sure the roots are fresh and have not dried out. Use a sharp knife to remove any encircling roots, or soft, mushy, or damaged parts. It always pays to order bareroot plants from a reliable nursery that will refund your money if the plant's roots are in poor condition upon arrival.

Bareroot plants are particularly vulnerable to drying out from sun and wind prior to planting. Once you have removed a plant from its protective shipping bag and examined it well, give it a thorough soaking, ideally for 30 to 60 minutes in tepid water just before planting. If you are unable to plant right away, soak each plant's roots, place them in plastic bags with moist mulch and store in a dark, cool place.

Careful planting is critical when working with bareroot plants. They should be planted in a hole two to three times as wide but no deeper than the height of the root ball. When digging, leave the soil high in the center of the hole to create a cone-like bottom. Place the plant with its crown at the top of the cone and then spread out its roots, like a skirt, in a circle around the cone. This allows the roots to grow evenly outward into the surrounding soil, which is yet another advantage of bareroot plants. If necessary, adjust the level of the cone to make sure the uppermost horizontal roots are situated just beneath the soil's surface. Finish by refilling the hole gradually, gently tamping down the compost-amended soil as you fill.

WATERING-IN AFTER PLANTING

Provide a crater around each plant and water thoroughly. For large shrubs and trees, it is a good idea to water when the hole is half filled and then again after it has filled and been firmly tamped. Newly planted trees and shrubs need 10 to 15 gallons of water when planted, depending upon the surrounding soil conditions. Follow up with a deep watering once a week if there is little or no rainfall.

Proper watering of newly planted perennials is key to their success. Roots need to be kept well supplied with water during this critical establishment period. Most plants require one inch of water a week while they are establishing themselves. After planting, check every other day depending upon the weather, and water accordingly. The simplest way to test moisture is to insert your finger into the soil. If the soil feels cool and moist one inch below the surface, there is no need to water. If you wish to be more precise, buy a water gauge or set up tin cans in different areas of the garden to get an exact reading of the weekly rainfall.

New, young plants have shallow root systems and because of this they need smaller and more frequent watering when freshly planted. After the first month, they should be watered less often but more deeply to encourage them to develop deep roots and build resistance to drought. Water wands are useful because they deposit water directly around individual plants right next to their root balls. This method is perfect for watering new plants that have been added to an established bed. It avoids wasting water on plants which may not need watering, or worse, may suffer from overwatering.

MULCHING AFTER PLANTING

In late spring, after making sure my garden beds have been conditioned and fed by compost, I order truckloads of light, fine-textured bark mulch. This is my favorite type of mulch because it adds a refined look to garden beds, acts as a slow-release soil conditioner and is reasonable to purchase. Fine-textured bark mulch (well-decomposed) takes very little nitrogen from the soil, and instead slowly releases its nutrients as it continues to decay. However, rough-textured bark mulch does rob the soil of significant amounts of nitrogen. This is because decomposing organisms need nitrogen to fuel their digestive activities as they break down large chunks of bark. I reserve rough bark or wood chips for our woodland garden where it defines paths and softens footsteps.

There are many other choices of mulch materials, such as cocoa hulls, pine needles, pea gravel, mushroom soil, chipped fruit wood, and so on. Mulch can be used as an esthetic tool to set the tone in a garden. I love to mulch our boxwood garden with a dark, coffee-colored humus we make from mixing Terry's precious worm compost into some of our outside compost. As I spread it lovingly under the boxwood, around all the herbs and at the foot of our weathered farm bell (To call

Mulch, if used properly, is a gardener's best friend.
It controls weeds, reduces evaporation of soil moisture,
promotes even soil temperatures and deters
erosion and soil compaction.

Terry if I am in need of his strong hands), the garden takes on an aura of days gone by. This is one of my favorite garden spaces; the smells and its almost palpable sweetness never cease to evoke the Maryland summers of my childhood.

A good rule of thumb is to maintain a top dressing of two to four inches of organic mulch throughout the year. Some well-intentioned gardeners suffocate plants by piling on huge amounts of mulch. A major peeve of mine is seeing piles of mulch heaped around the base of trees. (Gasoline stations seem to be one of the main culprits of this practice.) *Mulch should be kept three inches away from the crowns of perennials plants or trunks of trees to avoid rot diseases and to deter rodents from making homes immediately adjacent to trunks.*

Any new additions of mulch are best put on after the soil has thoroughly warmed in the spring and the soil microbes have become active in the decay process again. Also, it must wait until you have added compost, if your soil was in need of amending. (See March's chapter for in-depth discussions on this subject.)

Caution: Any mulch other than mature compost is best partly decomposed to avoid depleting the soil of nitrogen.

WHY, WHEN, AND HOW TO STAKE

Staking is a matter of choice and some gardeners refuse to buy plants which require any type of support. However, most serious perennial gardeners find that approach too restrictive and are quite willing to spend time staking to protect vulnerable plants. Many herbaceous plants, quite simply, do not have stiff enough stems to protect them from damage during strong seasonal storms.

Staking can also be used as a creative tool to enhance the overall aesthetics of a garden. With a bit of imagination and unique materials, you can turn what might otherwise be a tedious chore into an artistic adventure.

It is crucial to stake plants early on, before support is actually needed. Plants lose their natural beauty if they are stuffed into staking arrangements after they have grown too big, or worse, already suffered damage to their stems. To be more precise, staking should be carried out after the first flush of growth when plants have sturdy stems and before they form flower buds or reach full growth. Stakes should be no higher in the ground than three-quarters the height of the mature plant, except for large-flowering plants with weak stems. It will not take long for these stakes to become hidden by the rapidly maturing foliage of early summer.

Some staking can be avoided by placing plants with weak stems next to strong-stemmed plants. Light, airy plants like nepeta, can be intermingled with small perennial shrubs such as potentilla and daphne to create a charming, ethereal look. Another way to cut down on staking chores is to grow self-supporting tall plants. Coneflowers, daylilies and goldenrod are examples of tall, perennial plants that can be counted upon to withstand harsh storms and high winds.

Staking Multi-Stemmed Perennials

Stakes and string are one of the most versatile and universal methods for tying up and supporting plants during the growing season. Be sure to use jute string or other types of soft string to avoid cutting into plant stems. Wood and bamboo stakes are readily available and can be found at most garden centers in varying lengths and thicknesses. Metal hoops supported by three or four legs come in a variety of styles and are also available at most garden centers. For large, floppy plants like peonies, it is worth the extra expense of purchasing hoops which have metal latticework across their tops.

Keep your staking simple and hide the props as much as possible. Try to stake as naturally as possible by following the unique structure of each plant. Three to five stakes per plant works best, depending upon the size of the plant. Run the string around the perimeter of the plant (wrapping the string several times around each stake as you go). Follow up by crisscrossing the string across the top a number of times depending upon the size of the plant. This network of string allows a plant to grow upward and outward while maintaining its natural growth pattern. This type of staking is especially effective for large, numerous-stemmed perennials such as peonies and the huge-flowered *Hydrangea arborescens* 'Annabelle'. Summer rains often devastate these plants unless they are properly

staked early in the season. If they become badly flattened, they seldom recover, and remain an unsightly mess the rest of the season.

Staking Single-Stemmed Plants

Tall, thin poles made of bamboo are excellent supports for single-stemmed plants with spiked flower heads, such as delphiniums, or plants with a single heavy flower at the top of a stem like Asiatic lilies. Place the stake about an inch or so from the plant stem and push it into the ground far enough to make it stable, but no higher than two-thirds the height of the plant. Secure the stem to the stake by creating a loose figure eight with a plant tie. Keep the tie loose enough to allow some movement so it will not be too restrictive or damage the stem.

Other types of single-stemmed plant supports are made out of metal (usually covered with green plastic) and have an open loop at the top. These slide in easily next to the base of a plant, are fairly inconspicuous and can be used year after year.

Pea Staking

This type of staking is very popular in England and makes use of twiggy branches gleaned from various sources during the dormant season. The branches need to be kept about six inches shorter than the height of a mature plant and should be inserted into the ground when a plant is about eight to ten inches high. Pea stakes are the perfect support system for light and airy perennials such as baby's breath, asters, Artemisia lactiflora and cimicifuga. Experiment with different types of branch materials (hazel and fruit wood are excellent choices), always with an eye for interesting bark and branching patterns. I love to create interesting garden elements when carrying out my staking tasks at Muddy Creek.

Everything that grows or lives is
food for something else.

JUNE

Insects, Diseases, Prevention, and Treatments

id you know that a single handful of soil contains millions of bacteria, thousands of nematodes, hundreds of miles of fungi strands and a vast variety of insects? From my readings, I've learned that this amazing diversity of miniature life is constantly engaged in battle, and that most of the time the good guys win. Nature's scale seems to be tipped in life's favor, and at Muddy Creek I strive to respect that delicate balance.

In June, when the small creatures in my gardening world begin their dance of renewed life, I try to adopt a "laissez-faire" mind-set. Since most perennial gardens are virtually free of life-threatening pest and disease problems, chemical intervention is rarely necessary. And it is during this month that I realize what a large role my husband Terry plays in keeping our small ecosystem in balance. Thanks to his year-round bird-feeding efforts, a feathered army is constantly patrolling our summer gardens eating bugs, slugs, and snails. Also, beginning this month, he regularly stalks our gardens for Japanese beetles, which he sadistically drops into jars of soapy water. As I watch him poke his head into and around our tangled mass of porcelain vine, I realize how quickly these beetles bring out the darker side of this otherwise kind man.

My discussions in this chapter focus on natural, nontoxic methods for fighting pests and disease. But more importantly, they teach the importance and benefits of proper cultivation habits. The Eastern philosophy of preventative medicine seems to work just as well with plants as it does with humans.

ADOPT AN EASTERN-BASED GARDEN PHILOSOPHY

Plants serve important functions other than just looking perfect all the time. An imperfect garden better serves the natural world. At Muddy Creek, I've tried to create gardens that maintain a healthy, ecological balance of all creatures while also maintaining their ornamental beauty.

There is really little need to grow plants that require serious chemical controls since so many outstanding perennials are pest- and disease-resistant and not likely to suffer serious damage. Battling pests with toxic controls that aren't really necessary is only a waste of time and contributes to the destruction of our environment. Learn to tolerate a few holes or spots on leaves or even the loss of an entire plant some years. (Further discussions on chemical treatments are presented later in this chapter.)

 A perfect garden is one in which the imperfections of plants are in balance with the joys of hummingbirds and butterflies.

Don't despair if your favorite dog (or a neighbor's) digs up an entire section of the garden or an unexpected storm wreaks havoc just prior to a garden party. These are not major catastrophes in the grand scheme of things. Happy gardening is realizing that there will be times when you are powerless against the forces of nature or chance.

CULTIVATION PRACTICES FOR PEST AND DISEASE CONTROL

Proper soil and water management are the two most essential elements for successful perennial gardening. Poor cultivation practices often lead to stressed-out plants, making them more vulnerable to attack from disease and insects. Always try to learn your plants' needs for soil, water, and sunlight, and site them accordingly for optimal health. For instance, an azalea misplaced in full sun will experience constant stress and will be more prone to ravage from insects.

As I'll discuss in August, it is always best to do any overhead watering early in the morning. This allows the sun and air to dry off wet foliage and goes a long way toward preventing fungal diseases.

In plants, as well as in animals, the first defense against attack is maintaining general health and vitality. Dead leaves and decaying plant parts often harbor disease organisms, and they also provide safe hiding places for slugs and other damaging insects. Many of these pests can overwinter in some life form or another in the protective climate of this debris, so the best preventative medicine is to keep gardens free of dead or decayed material. Always bag or burn all parts of diseased plants, including twigs, flower heads, fruits and seeds. *Only put healthy garden remains in the compost pile!* And last, but not least, avoid the pitfall of smothering a plant with too much mulch. To avoid rot diseases, always keep mulch three inches away from crowns and stems.

Space plants so they receive optimal amounts of air circulation to help guard against insects and disease. Bad bugs love to hide in foliage away from predators, the drying sun and wind. Fungi and bacteria thrive and multiply faster in the dark, damp undersides of leaves. Deadhead and cut back dying plant parts throughout the growing season to constantly create new openings in the garden canopy.

Learn to cultivate plants that are inherently less prone to being eaten, such as rhododendrons, daylilies, magnolias and weigelas, to name just a few. Also, make it a policy to grow only as many leafy species as you can knowledgably care for, which includes becoming familiar with the specific problems of each plant. Be sure to include plenty of pollen or nectar-producing perennials in order to attract beneficial insects. These plants will help keep a favorable balance of good to bad bugs in your garden environment.

Plant a variety of species. The diversity you create will guard against the possibility of losing large sections of a garden at any one time, since many pests and diseases are species specific. Try to embrace the smart garden practice of purchasing plants from modern growers who continually market new varieties of disease- and pest-resistant plants. And never be meek about removing from your gardens troublesome plants that come under attack year after year. At Muddy Creek, it took me three years of battling aphids and its accompanying black soot disease on my honeysuckle vines before I decided to rip them all out and burn them. It makes little sense to spend precious garden hours dealing with the same sickly plants year after year when there are many other choice perennials to choose from.

> The majority of perennial plants are immune to most diseases. Susceptibility to a particular pathogen is the exception, not the norm!

June is the month to begin close-up observation of each garden plant on a regular basis for the remainder of the growing season. In areas with dormant seasons, late spring is a time when plants have ample supplies of water, pollen, nectar and tender, young foliage. Due to this abundance, plant organisms that are dependent upon other plant life for survival are also at a peak. Just as in humans, detecting problems early is the key to maintaining health. You should have a head start, since ideally you will have just finished digging and composting and should already know the status of most of the plants in your gardens.

For every bad bug, fungus, or bacterium, there are several beneficial organisms ready to defend against them. These countless, amicable predators and parasites are continually at work keeping pests and disease under control, greatly lowering the amount of human intervention required. It also helps to know that as flowers go by and foliage becomes brittle and bitter, plants become much less appealing. So it is mostly downhill for the bad guys as the season progresses.

PLANT DISEASES AND THEIR SYMPTOMS

This month, begin to diligently check your gardens for early signs of disease. Keen observations at this time can pick up early symptoms of a disease before it becomes too entrenched. If left undiscovered, there may be major consequences later in the growing season. This is the time to call on human troops for field assistance before the enemy gets a foothold!

When a disease organism disturbs normal plant function or leads to abnormal growth patterns in a plant, it can usually be recognized and diagnosed by specific symptoms. These symptoms may appear suddenly, as in certain clematis wilt diseases; but quite often they hide inside a plant's tissues or roots long before any obvious symptoms appear. Root infections in trees which cause branches to die back gradually over a period of many years are prime examples of hidden enemies.

Classifying and identifying plant diseases can be difficult because many of them are microscopic and undetectable to the naked eye. Laboratory testing is the only sure way to make positive identification, but such testing is time-consuming, costly and often tricky if the specimen isn't in the right life-cycle stage. Therefore, a strong offense remains the best defense for the home gardener. The preventative and curative garden practices laid out earlier in this chapter remain the safest and most practical way to manage and control disease organisms in the home perennial garden.

Viral diseases do not usually kill plants, but they make very distinct mottled or mosaic patterns (usually light green or yellow) on the leaves. They often cause plants to grow in odd shapes or develop puckered or distorted leaves. Plant viruses can only grow in the cells of their host plant, but they can be carried from host to host by vectors, such as sap-sucking insects, contaminated tools or hands. Scientists know very little about plant viruses and have no cures as of yet, so the best way to protect the perennial garden against them is to keep down the populations of sap-sucking insects and burn or bag all diseased plants or plant parts.

Bacterial diseases are even more difficult to control in plants than in humans. Few plant antibiotics exist and they are expensive and impractical for home perennial gardens. Bacterial organisms are single-celled and reproduce by cellular division. They can also reproduce by creating resting spores which overwinter by hiding in soil, plant tissue or garden debris. These resting spores remain dormant until the warmth of spring allows them to become active again and re-infect plants. Bacterial disease is characterized by holes or spots in leaves. The best defense against a bad bacterium is to remove all diseased plants or plant parts from the garden immediately upon discovery and to practice cleanliness throughout the garden year.

Fungi are the largest and most diverse group of infectious disease organisms that attack plants. Again, identification in the laboratory can be difficult if the right life-cycle stage is not present. They also can exist through cold winters by producing dormant spores which hide out waiting to become active at the right time in the spring. Fungi grow over time, so by the time you see leaves coated with

white spores of powdery mildew or red, black or brown spores of rust disease, the fungus may have been growing within the plant for at least a few weeks. Fungi attack certain plants more than others and in many cases fungi survive year after year to continually attack susceptible plants. Delphiniums, phlox, peonies, roses and hollyhock are just a few of the perennial plants that are under continual threat from fungal diseases.

MOST COMMON DISEASES
OF PERENNIAL PLANTS

Black Spot: This fungal disease is one of the most common diseases that attacks the rose family. The first symptoms are dark brown or black spots on leaves that can be up to half an inch in diameter. These spots are surrounded by  yellowing tissue, and as these discolored areas increase in size, the disease may cause the leaves to die and fall off. If allowed to spread unchecked, it can completely defoliate the plant. The spores overwinter on dead leaves, but they can also hide out on stems in bud scales or stem lesions. Simply removing dead and diseased plant debris does not always wipe out this fungus. In the spring, dormant spores that have overwintered awaken to begin the disease's renewed life cycle. The only sure way to avoid this disease in the perennial garden without the use of toxic chemicals is to grow disease-resistant roses.

Botrytis Blight: This is a fungal disease that attacks peonies, cranesbill and certain other perennial plants. It is an airborne disease with a proclivity for plants such as red-flowering peonies that contain high levels of carbohydrates. These excessive carbohydrate amounts create sticky sugars on leaf surfaces which seem to be a big attraction for this blight disease. The fungus looks like a grayish-brown growth on buds and often appears fuzzy. An infected plant's leaves exhibit discolored  patches and its flowers become brown and droopy and tend to drop off when touched. To avoid contaminating the soil from these fallen flowers, make it a priority to deadhead all flower heads before they can become infected. Also, since this fungus over-winters on infected garden debris, make it a point to cut all peonies to ground level early in the fall to further combat this disease. If you give your peonies plenty of space for air to circulate around them and always practice good hygiene, you will probably avoid this disease altogether!

Mildew (Downy and Powdery): The main symptom, a white, powdery coating on leaves, is the same for both types of this fungal disease. A variety of plants are susceptible, among which are roses, lilacs, phlox and bee balm. It is helpful to know that there are many specific kinds of mildew fungi, each of which is plant

specific. A mildew that attacks roses won't harm bee balm and vice versa. These fungal diseases often disfigure a plant and make it unsightly, but are not usually lethal. However, their presence can weaken plants, making them more susceptible to other problems. Downy mildew is less conspicuous of the two, but is more of a threat because it has the potential to seriously cripple or kill plants. Downy mildew comes early in the season when conditions are wetter and cooler. On the other hand, powdery mildew likes warm, humid weather and cool nights and is always ready to feed on plants when the conditions are suitable. Both types of mildew disease can be deterred by avoiding overhead watering of vulnerable plants and by buying disease-resistant plants.

Rot Disease: This disease includes crown, stem and root rots and can be caused by a wide range of fungi, or in some cases by bacteria. Sometimes it is simply a physiological disorder resulting from excessive soil moisture in the immediate vicinity of the diseased plant. Its symptoms are a general discoloration of leaves and wilting of above-ground plant parts, brown or black rotting crown and root tissue, and in severe cases, the complete collapse of a plant, if not caught early enough. To get rid of rot, cut off all damaged parts of affected plants or totally destroy severely affected plants. Sometimes it makes sense to move vulnerable plants to new, uninfected sites in the garden. Plants are particularly susceptible to infection

if they have been over- or under-watered or incorrectly planted. Check the soil regularly for drainage and make sure excessive or incorrect mulching practices are not causing the problem. Always take the time to rid your garden of any poorly drained areas by adding copious amounts of compost.

Rust: This is a fungal disease that is easy to detect and identify because it forms a distinctive rusty coating on foliage. Luckily, it is rarely a serious problem for perennial gardens. Some susceptible plants are roses, hollyhock and cedar. This disease can go back and forth between vulnerable plants and trees for years on

end. For example, Muddy Creek has many cedar and fruit trees in surrounding meadows and woodlands. These trees are constantly under attack from rust fungi, and as a result, they continually spread this disease. Since it is impossible and undesirable to eliminate all of these trees, I practice the preventative measures discussed in this chapter to keep this fungus at bay in my perennial gardens.

Sooty Mold: Aphids and other sap-sucking insects drop sticky, honey-like droppings called honeydew as they chew on foliage. Sooty mold, a black-colored mold (non-parasitic fungus) often grows on these droppings, which is quite unsightly but is harmless to the health of the plant. To rid a plant of this problem, spray with a soapy water mixture to rinse off the honeydew and accompanying mold. (See recipe at the end of this chapter.) Follow up with regular water sprays to keep the sap-sucking pests off the plant.

Wilt: This is a soil-born fungal disease very difficult to detect in its early stages. Some of these fungi can survive many years in the soil without a host and after silently entering a plant through its root system, often lead to its death. Early signs

of the disease are leaf yellowing and wilting of plant stems. It is wise to buy wilt-resistant or wilt-tolerant plants because there is a high fatality rate in susceptible plants due to the difficulties of early detection. Certain clematis are highly susceptible to wilt disease, but there are plenty of resistant varieties to grow in their stead. Always clean up and destroy all infected plant parts immediately upon discovery of this disease!

THE MOST COMMON GARDEN PESTS
AND METHODS OF CONTROL

Aphids: These are tiny, soft-bodied, sap-sucking insects with needlelike noses. Some have wings and others do not, and depending on the species, they range in color from green, red and yellow all the way to brown and black. They vary in length from one-sixteenth to three-eighths of an inch long.

Problems and Symptoms: The naked eye can see clusters of these insects on foliage, especially on the underside of leaves and on flower heads. Aphids suck sap from leaves and large infestations can cause blooms to become stunted or deformed. Furthermore, they can act as vectors of diseases as they move from infected plants to healthy ones.

Control: Always use water sprays as your first method of attack and follow up with a soapy wash when necessary. Make sure your garden has plenty of plants that attract aphid-eating insects, such as green lacewings and ladybird beetles. (Refer to references in the December chapter to purchase additional amounts of these beneficial insects and to learn which plants attract them.)

 **Borers:** Borers resemble small worms in appearance and are usually less than one inch in length. Several types of beetle and caterpillar larvae are included in this group.

Problems and Symptoms: Borers tunnel into the wood, roots or stems of certain trees and plants, weakening the plant by cutting off the nutrient flow, and thereby making it more susceptible to disease. Signs to look for are dead bark, sawdust piles and poor performance overall.

Control: Crush by hand or foot any borers that you see and prune any infested plants to within a few inches of the crown, removing any remaining brown or curled leaves at the base. Cut off and destroy infected limbs of trees, and purchase parasitic nematodes to inject into the remaining borer holes. Borer eggs can over-winter in garden debris, so it is particularly important to remove all garden debris in the vicinity. Since German bearded iris are highly susceptible to borer damage, try planting Siberian iris in their stead. Make sure that plants with rhizomes are not planted too low in the ground. If the sun can't help dry them, it is easy for rot disease to set in following a borer attack.

Japanese Beetles: These hard-backed pests are blue-green in color with coppery wings. In their larva stage they are fat, white and curved, measuring a little longer than the one-half inch adults.

Problems and Symptoms: Adult beetles seem to have an affinity for certain plants, such as roses and porcelain vine. They seldom kill plants but often desecrate the foliage by feeding profusely once the larvae have matured into adults. Their presence in large numbers on individual plants and the unsightly holes they cause in leaves, can ruin the aesthetic appeal of the plants they are feeding upon. They tend to weaken plants, making them more vulnerable to disease.

Control: Try to check infested plants regularly, especially early in the day or after dark when the beetles are very lethargic. Hold a can of soapy water under each group of bugs and knock them off individually, or gently jiggle the branch to get large numbers at one time. This method of control is very effective if carried out on a daily basis, hopefully by one of your human worker bees. Enlist beneficials by treating your lawn with milky spore disease (bacterial microorganisms) or parasitic nematodes, both of which attack the larva stage of these pests.

Mites: This group includes a variety of tiny, often microscopic insects that feed by sucking juices from plant foliage. Mites vary in color from tans and grays to greens and reds.

Problems and Symptoms: Some mites, such as spider mites, tend to feed on the undersides of leaves. As they suck on plant juices, they leave behind a telltale, silk webbing which may be visible upon close examination. They cause leaves to discolor or drop off, stunt or distort growth and in general cause a lack of vigor in plants they prey upon. In severe situations leaves curl up and fall off, sometimes leaving a completely denuded plant.

Control: Remove all discolored or dead leaves from infested plants and clean up all garden debris, particularly in the fall, to destroy breeding places. Cut off all foliage to ground level after flowering if you have an infestation problem. Most plants will grow their foliage back later in the season, but if not, they surely will the following season. Always be on early lookout for infestations, and upon discovery, blast them off with a strong hose spray or a soapy wash.

Nematodes: These unsegmented, worm-like animals are mostly microscopic and live in soil or as parasites within plant tissue. Nematodes feed on plants by sucking sap from plant tissue with their piercing mouthparts. They also act as vectors in spreading plant viruses, in the same manner as aphids and other sap-sucking insects.

Problems and Symptoms: Since nematodes live in the soil or within plant tissue, it is difficult for most home gardeners to determine their presence. Infected plants usually exhibit brown patterns in their leaves and may experience distorted or stunted growth, which can sometimes kill the plant.

Control: It is important to rid the perennial garden of infected plants, since chemical controls are not a viable means of attack. In six years of gardening at Muddy Creek, I have never had a serious problem with any destructive nematodes. Practicing the preventative measures of proper soil and water management truly are the best way to protect your home gardens from attack.

Scales: These are very tiny insects with protective shells of varying shapes and colors. The female adults are brown, flattened and oval-shaped, while adult males are tiny, two-winged insects. The females are about one-fifth of an inch long and live by sucking juices from plant stems and bark.

Problems and Symptoms: A heavy infestation of these insects can reduce a plant's vigor and even kill it, if undetected in the early stages of attack. They leave sticky, honey-like droppings similar to deposits left by aphids. But unlike aphids, they do not move once they have found a desirable feeding place. They cling to leaves and stems, using their shells as shields. To the inexperienced eye, they look like small bumps.

Control: It is important to be on regular lookout for scale insects in order to discover them early. If they are allowed to get a foothold, they can totally encrust large sections of plants or trees. If some branches die back, remove all affected parts immediately and dispose of them by burning or bagging. Make sure your garden ecosystem has plenty of ladybird beetles because they love to dine on scales. Purchase some extras if you seem to have a deficiency, and remember to keep the garden well planted with perennials that attract beneficial insects. Use a homemade oil spray to smother large colonies of these hard-bodied pests. (See recipe at the end of this chapter.)

Snails and Slugs: These are slimy, soft-bodied mollusks, some of which are equipped with hard, protective shells. Adults range in color from tan to black and range in size from one-eighth to one inch. They thrive in dark, dank garden spots, where they breed and hide in mulch and debris.

Problems and Symptoms: These nocturnal creatures love to feed on decaying plant debris or tender leaves in the cool of the night or in rainy weather. They use their raspy mouths to scrape holes in foliage and often leave a slimy trail behind on the foliage which allows you to differentiate them from caterpillars. The damage is almost always within the leaf margin between veins rather than on the edges. These pests love hosta plants, particularly ones with thin, tender leaves, and especially those which touch the ground.

Control: The damage snails and slugs do is mostly cosmetic, and these pests can be kept to tolerable levels by hand-picking and/or by placing saucers of beer for them to drown in or upside down grapefruit halves for you to find them hiding under. Another effective defense is to scatter piles of rough sand or diatomaceous earth (DE) around vulnerable plants to kill or deter them as they try to crawl across the sharp barrier.

NATURAL METHODS FOR CONTROLLING PESTS AND DISEASES

Adding high quality, properly cured compost to garden beds each spring introduces copious amounts of new microbes to your soil. These tiny creatures promote rapid removal of pathogenic spores and prey on plant-damaging insects as they break down the organic matter in the compost. In other words, compost added to the soil not only supplies all the vital plant nutrients as it breaks down, but it also is a major boost to plant health by providing a healthier environment for decay- and disease-fighting creatures.

In home gardens, enlist birds to help hold nature in balance. Very few birds are all bad, and most garden varieties earn their keep by eating four times their weight in bugs each day. Provide plenty of shelter and sustenance by planting

> The primary defense tools in home perennial gardens
> should be manual or mechanical: feet, hands,
> water and organic sprays, pruners and traps.

evergreen trees, feeding birds during the lean, winter months and keeping bird-baths filled. Birds do very little damage to the garden themselves, but are worth their weight in gold for the predators they consume daily. To protect fruit crops, place light netting over blueberries and other edible berry plants as the crop nears ripening time.

Encourage good insects (beneficials) throughout your garden and surrounding ecosystem by planting a wide variety of plants for food and shelter. Nectar and pollen are valuable food sources for many desirable insects besides bees. The goldenrod plant attracts more than 75 different species of beneficials. Some of my favorite insect-attracting plants are asters, butterfly bush, catmint, chamomile, hyssop, lavender, oregano, thyme and veronica.

The majority of insects in nature are beneficial to the perennial gardener. Beneficial insects break down organic matter, pollinate, and prey on other more damaging insects. *Keep in mind that only a small portion of insects do damage in the garden!* For example, ladybird beetles are vociferous aphid consumers. These good bugs consume large numbers of bad bugs in their
daily diets. Always try to keep the balance high on the side of the good guys, since the bad insects can breed much more prolifically if their natural enemies have been eliminated. (Check the references in the December chapter for places to purchase beneficial bugs targeted for specific bad insects in your garden.)

As mentioned earlier, an effective and fun method of trapping slugs, grubs or snails is to place saucers of beer at soil level in hosta beds. These creatures seem to share the human attraction for this intoxicant and happily climb into the saucers only to drown from their folly.

Ants often like to make their homes underneath perennial plants. Large colonies often dry out and weaken plants because plants tend to rise up in the soil as ants develop their chambers. The best attack is to buy a root nozzle for your water hose so you can drown the ants in their chambers. When the nozzle is correctly inserted into the chambers, it will feel as though the probe is touching sugar cubes. This treatment successfully kills ant colonies by flooding their egg chambers, but if you're not careful, it can also drown the plant. To avoid leaving behind a disease-attracting swamp, try to carry out this treatment when the surrounding soil is on the dry side. It is important to catch an ant colony early and keep it on the run; otherwise, you may lose an entire plant once the ants have become entrenched and the plant has lost too much moisture.

Spend some fun hours in the winter reading about caterpillars. Learn how to identify desirable larvae that will mature to grace your gardens with butterflies in the summer time. This knowledge will allow you to pick off and kill the destructive caterpillars while leaving the beneficials unharmed.

Other common and troublesome garden pests include voles, mice, squirrels, chipmunks, rabbits and deer, to name just a few. Protecting perennial garden from these larger animal pests is a book of its own. At Muddy Creek, the combination of two active dogs, plus coyotes and foxes in the woods, seems to keep the perennial gardens relatively unscathed by rodents and other four-footed pests.

If all else fails, adjust your plant choices! Try growing disease-resistant plants such as the white phlox, *P. paniculata* 'David', old-fashioned shrub roses, or monkshood instead of delphinium, and in general avoid any perennial plants

that require yearly fungicide spraying to keep them disease free. As stated earlier in this book, there are many trouble-free plants to substitute for disease-prone plants. Polluting our planet by yearly chemical spraying in the home perennial garden seems environmentally irresponsible. The planet would benefit immensely if more gardeners could learn to embrace this philosophy.

REASONS TO AVOID CHEMICAL TREATMENTS

Inorganic (synthetic) pesticides are foreign objects to the soil and plants. They can have many adverse effects on the natural environment. Inorganic chemical controls work systemically and make all parts of a plant poisonous, including the pollen or nectar, which many beneficial insects eat at some point in their lives. The roots also absorb some of these toxins, which then directly affect the surrounding soil creatures, the good as well as the bad. Scientists know that beneficial soil fungi and bacteria are clearly important in contributing to plant health, but they are just beginning to understand exactly how this relationship works. For instance, some beneficial fungi symbiotically team up with roots by increasing the roots' ability to absorb nutrients. In return, the roots enable the fungi to absorb carbohydrates for fuel. *It is vital to protect these plant allies*!

Also, plant diseases are adept at building resistance to specific products after too much exposure, just as many human diseases build resistance to certain antibiotics. So, try to be just as cautious using inorganic pesticides as you are with human prescription drugs.

The use of harsh chemical pest and disease controls on a regular basis can expose your family and immediate surroundings to a cumulative buildup of toxic chemicals. Choose to manage your ecosystem naturally, not poison it!

It is always best to attempt to properly identify the culprit before indiscriminately spraying. And, most importantly, try to treat the primary cause of the health problem, not the symptoms. Rot diseases usually are the result of poor plant hygiene or saturated, unhealthy soils. Correct any sloppy garden habits by cleaning up debris, improving drainage and making sure mulches are well back from crowns and stems.

Keep in mind, that even though a product is naturally derived, it still may be toxic to a certain degree to some plants in your ecosystem, especially to beneficials. Perennial plants have very tough cell walls and their internal, cellular fluids contain natural insecticide compounds. It is best to rely on the innate abilities of most perennial plants to resist infection or attack, supported by preventative and curative methods described in this chapter before ever intervening with environmentally unfriendly chemicals.

ORGANIC INSECT AND DISEASE CONTROL PRODUCTS

Bacillus thuringienisis (**BT**): This insecticide consists of a group of bacteria that infects insects. BT already exists in the soil naturally, and it acts by producing protein crystals that are toxic to specific insects. It is effective on some leaf-eating pests, and even though it is very slow-acting, it breaks down quickly in the environment. BT's negatives are that over-use will allow insects to build up immunities, and it may kill future butterflies and other beneficials along with targeted pests.

Milky Spore: This product works by introducing milky spore, a bacterial disease, into the soil specifically to attack pests such as Japanese beetles in their soil- dwelling stages. It seems to be fairly benign to the environment in all other respects.

Diatomaceous Earth (**DE**): This powder-like dust is made of silicate skeletons of tiny, ancient, water creatures called diatoms, which are mined in certain parts of the world. They are similar to ground glass and work by cutting into the waxy coats of insects, causing them to dry out and die. DE is easy for humans to handle while spreading on the ground around infested plants, is nontoxic and

leaves no harmful residue. The only negative is that beneficials are also vulnerable to its lethal, cutting edges.

Insecticidal Soaps: These consist of certain fatty acids that are mainly toxic to soft-bodied insects, such as aphids, mealy bugs, spider mites, and whiteflies, but can also be effective against some harder-bodied insects, such as Japanese beetles. Soap insecticides act fast and have little effect on non-targeted insects, making them the only really safe pesticide for spraying.

Recipe for Insecticidal Soap

Mix two tablespoons of Murphy's liquid soap with one gallon of softened water. Be aware that water which contains high levels of dissolved minerals diminishes the effectiveness of soap sprays.

Insecticidal soaps may be harmful to aquatic invertebrates, so avoid using around water where there is a potential to harm aquatic life. The other concern in using these soaps is that they can burn the leaves of certain plants, especially when temperatures are high.

Glyphosate (Roundup®, Rodeo®): Glyphosate is a clear, odorless liquid chemical used as a non-selective herbicide which has gained wide acceptance among conservationists. Since it is ingested systemically, it must be applied carefully in order to avoid injuring nearby plants and soil. Always spray on a windless day taking care to treat only the targeted plants. Try using a brush to coat the leaves when you have a small amount of plant material to eradicate. This product works best in the spring when leaves are still small and less glyphosate is needed to kill the plant. Bishop's weed and burdock are two examples of highly invasive plants that justify the use of this inorganic herbicide.

Organic Oils: These summertime oil sprays are more diluted than dormant sprays and are effective in controlling scales, mealy bugs and a number of other bugs and fungi. Organic oils such as canola and jojoba are used as the base ingredient rather than environmentally unfriendly, petroleum-based oils.

Recipe for Organic Oil Spray

Mix one cup of oil with one tablespoon of liquid soap. Stir well and add one tablespoon of this mixture to one quart of water and spray as needed.

Caring for a garden, is in fact,
the essence of gardening.

JULY

Deadheading, Pinching, and Cutting Back

uly at Muddy Creek marks the end of the first third of the growing season. Fresh spring foliage is looking down-trodden, early flowering perennials and shrubs have finished their spring fling, and the dog days of summer are upon us. Much of what is to happen in my gardens for the remainder of the season will be directly determined by my summer pruning choices. I can actually feel the manipulative side of my personality returning.

My first summers at Muddy Creek were often filled with anguish as I watched our perennial beds slide into chaotic eyesores. I often coped with this summer ugliness by escaping to Martha's Vineyard where I could forget about the gardens altogether. In my ignorance, I mistakenly thought that all perennial gardens experienced an inevitable summertime decline. However, as I learned about the miracles of deadheading and cutting back, my outlook began to change. Now, I wait until fall for trips away because I simply can't bear to miss the faded beauty of my late summer gardens.

This past fall, after many years of tending my perennials, the gardens were so lovely to behold that I actually enjoyed them more than I had earlier in the season. Re-blooming foxglove and mullein were weaving their way amongst the coneflowers, nepeta and Russian sage, creating patterns more exotic than the finest Turkish mosaic. Even though our late season gardens are less showy, their muted, understated hues always provide the perfect transition into the quietude of autumn.

DEADHEADING

This summertime pruning chore involves the removal of faded blossoms from a plant, partly for aesthetic purposes, but also to prolong or promote bloom, to control growth or to prevent plants from setting seed.

Gardeners often maximize the aspect of the plant that made them choose it. If it is blossoms, they do their best to stimulate a second flowering.

Reasons for Deadheading

Regular deadheading can extend the bloom time of perennial plants by several weeks and often stimulates a second flowering later in the season. Perennials spend a great deal of energy during the growing season producing flowers and setting seed for self-perpetuation. Deadheading diverts this preservation energy back to a plant's vegetative and root growth needs. By thwarting these first seed-ripening efforts, gardeners can stimulate perennial plants to begin this process all over again.

The overall appearance of a perennial garden is greatly enhanced if spent flowers are regularly removed because decaying bloom material becomes a distraction to the eye. Plants which bear large flower heads can ruin the look of a bed when the flowers are dying and weighing the plant down. Also, old, decaying plant material can become a health hazard by attracting bugs and/or disease to the garden. Peonies, especially some of the red flowering varieties, should be deadheaded immediately after flowering. Their mushy, spent flower heads are particularly disease-prone, and if left on plants, can attract fungal diseases to their soft stem tissues.

The lifespan of some biennial plants can be prolonged by several years if aggressively deadheaded. Besides stimulating new growth and re-bloom, biennials such as foxglove may come back a third or fourth year if their flower stalks are removed in a timely manner during both flowering periods. This prevents plants from using all of their energy to ripen seeds.

Self-seeding is prevented if all seed heads are removed during the deadheading process. However, it is each gardener's prerogative to decide which plants should be left un-deadheaded in order to self sow. Some plants such as *datura* (angel's trumpet) and *Euphorbia marginata* (snow-on-the-mountain) are annuals in northern climates but act like perennials if left to self-seed. They reliably produce an abundant supply of new seedlings each spring. Others, like columbine, are short-lived perennials but perpetuate themselves by self-sowing. Learn to be selective, and remember that with prolific breeders it is usually best to allow only a few deadheads to remain. Pay close attention to such factors as how far seeds fall from a parent plant. (Do they stay close at hand or ride with the winds?) By limiting these multitudes of scattered seeds, the next season's weeding time can be greatly reduced. After several years of observation, most gardeners learn to access the net worth of each type of seed head and adopt maintenance programs that meet their specific goals.

Note that most herbaceous perennial seedlings grow true to type, but seedlings from cultivars sometimes hybridize into new varieties. Thus, inconsistent patterns can develop whereby original cultivars give way to new plants which may not be as desirable as the originals. On the other hand, you may end up with a pleasant surprise! If you are by nature adaptable, you may decide to let nature do its thing and actually revel in the unplanned, cottage-style garden that sometimes develops.

Birds love to eat seeds, and a great deal of their vital food sources are supplied by seed heads left in the garden. They particularly like the seeds of blue globe thistle, coneflower and sunflower. Since these plants re-seed prolifically and can take over beds, try deadheading two-thirds of a stand, leaving one-third

for the birds. As an extra bonus, these attractive seed heads lend subtle beauty to the bare winter landscape.

Grooming and tidying up can be some of the best times spent in the garden. Get in tune with your particular tastes and needs by carefully observing your perennial beds throughout several growing seasons. Settle down and use your common sense regarding these chores. If done on a regular basis, time spent deadheading can be quiet, meditative work and may actually become one of your favorite garden chores.

Correct Times to Deadhead

Deadheading is a continuous process, beginning with the first flowers of spring and not ending until the first killing frost. Try to keep up with this ongoing task so you can enjoy the process and not become overwhelmed.

A plant's age greatly influences its deadheading requirements. There is often a grace period with first-year plants because most of their energy is directed toward establishing themselves in their new home. By the second year, their root systems will be established and they can begin concentrating their energies on flower and seed production.

Deadheading chores will need to be carried out for a longer period of time in the spring and early summer if the weather has been cool and moist. Conversely, extremely warm, dry weather or damaging storms shorten this initial deadheading period.

CATEGORIES OF PLANTS FOR DEADHEADING

Most herbaceous perennial plants flower in three basic patterns and it is important to understand their differences in order to deadhead correctly. The categories listed here are not scientifically based, but are presented to serve as loose guidelines from a gardener's point of view.

Group A: The majority of perennial plants fall into this category and are characterized by bearing one or two flowers on individual stems. Usually the center flower opens first, with the buds on lower, side shoots opening later. Some examples of this type of plant are achillea (yarrow), aquilegia (columbine), aster, campanula (bellflower) and salvia.

Method of Deadheading

Use hand-held pruners to remove each faded stalk just above a secondary stem, bud or leaf. After all the side shoots have flowered, cut the plant back to its basal leaves or to a few inches from the ground. This can be tedious and time-consuming. If time is at a premium, it is perfectly fine to shear these plants back instead of cutting off each individual stem over a period of a few weeks. This technique may cause you to lose a few of the last crop of blossoms, but the plant usually rejuvenates and re-blooms later in the season.

Group B: These perennials have many flowers clustered on one stem or on short side stems. Most plants in this group are best relieved of their blossoms after the entire group has finished its bloom period. Examples of plants in this group are ajuga, bergenia, daylily, coral bells, hosta, Oriental and Asiatic lilies, Jacob's ladder and penstemon.

Methods of Deadheading

Many of these types have a large quantity of smaller, individual flowers which require you to wait until all the flowers have gone by before removal of the stem. Do this in the same manner as group A, by cutting back to the first set of healthy leaves below the spent flowers or to the basal leaves.

Some of these types have large individual flowers which should be pinched or snapped off as soon as they have gone by. Be extra careful when removing spent

daylily blossoms because it is easy to damage or knock off nearby flower buds. The thumbnail pressed against the forefinger is one of the best tools for this job. The stem is then cut to its base above the first set of leaves after all the flowers have bloomed. Note that with lilies, this chore is mainly for aesthetic purposes except in the case of a few, such as the daylily, *Hemerocallis* 'Stella d'Oro', which brightens late summer gardens with a second show of golden-yellow flowers if religiously deadheaded.

Oriental and Asiatic lilies have a special requirement once you have removed the large, spent flower heads. It is important to leave the remaining tall stalks and their leaves for removal later on in the season when all the stalks have died back naturally. These stalks and leaves are needed throughout the growing season to send food stores to the bulbs below to supply energy for the following season. However, older clumps with many stalks can give up a few for flower arrangements without unduly damaging the plant.

Group C: Perennial plants in this group are characterized by flower heads which form a raceme (flowers which grow along a single spike, either directly on the spike or on very short stems off the spike). They are easy to identify because the peak of the spike continues to come into flower as the blossoms lower down on the raceme die and develop seed pods. Some typical examples of plants in this third category are hollyhock, foxglove, mullein and veronica.

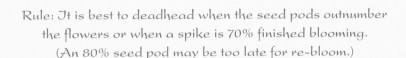

Rule: It is best to deadhead when the seed pods outnumber
the flowers or when a spike is 70% finished blooming.
(An 80% seed pod may be too late for re-bloom.)

Methods of Deadheading

Gardeners should use their judgment in deciding when to cut off dying flower stalks. These flower heads look very unsightly as they go by and can distract from the overall beauty of neighboring plants. A general rule to follow is to cut them when there is a greater length of seed pod on the spike than fresh flowers. It is best to cut sooner rather than later to allow plenty of time for a second bloom to occur before the season's end. The second set of blooms will be smaller and the plant will be shorter, but this practice provides welcome color and fresh foliage later in the summer.

PINCHING

This is a type of plant treatment conducted in spring and early summer. It involves removing the growing tips and first set of leaves (usually about a two-inch length from each shoot) from many of a plant's branches. Pinching is one of the best-known forms of summer pruning.

Reasons to Pinch

One of the major reasons gardeners pinch back perennial plants is to promote fuller plants. As apical buds and leaves are pinched from stems, side buds are stimulated to form new branches, which results in bushier, less leggy plants.

This practice is best suited for herbaceous perennial plants whose natural growth patterns are multi-branched. It is of no benefit to plants growing from rhizomes, bulbs, corms or to plants with basal or rosette-forming foliage.

Another reason to pinch is to affect the flowering time of perennial plants. Depending upon when and how you pinch back a plant, it is possible to delay, extend or stagger bloom times. Plants pinched back early in the growing season (with the exception of those pinched very early on) will flower later than normal and will produce smaller, more abundant blooms.

Pinching back is beneficial to first-year plants, which are unnaturally tall and leggy (with long distances between leaf nodes). Sometimes this task is difficult to carry out, especially when you are forced to remove flowers that are in bloom or about to open. It is important to remind yourself that in no time at all, this vital pruning will stimulate lots of branching and healthy, new growth. Conversely, if you neglect to pinch back these unattractive, leggy plants, they may continue to exhibit the same undesirable growth patterns all season long.

Pinching is an effective means of keeping prolific growers in bounds. Certain plants can grow too big for their allotted garden space, especially in garden zones with mild winters and long growing seasons. A few pinches early in the growing season ensures that a plant won't overrun its neighbors. Unfortunately, few gardeners take full advantage of this valuable pruning technique. If practiced knowledgeably, it can greatly enhance the habit and flowering effects of numerous perennials. For example, certain asters, such as the tall New England aster (*A. novae-angliae*) have natural growth patterns which produce tall, leafless stems with flower heads perched atop unsightly legs. By pinching or cutting back (to be discussed next), these untidy giants can be encouraged to grow lower and bushier, eliminating the bare stem problem.

> *Summer pruning can transform a good garden into a great one.*

The practice of pinching can be a good alternative for the inexperienced or timid gardener who might be hesitant to cut back large portions of plants and feels safer pinching off small bits at a time. Physiologically, the practices of pinching and cutting back bear the same results, so gardeners can choose the method which best suits them.

Timing and Techniques

The most available tool for pinching back herbaceous perennials is a gardener's thumb and forefinger. The tip of a plant is pinched off by a quick, but firm pressing together of these two digits (some gardeners keep one thumbnail longer just for this purpose), which severs it cleanly from the plant. Try to make each pinch just above a node with a top bud pointing outwards. This pinching technique makes a softer, more natural look than cutting with man-made tools.

However, when faced with pinching back large quantities of plant material, it is often more efficient to use hand-held pruners. Entire handfuls of stems can be grabbed together in one hand while the other hand snips off the tips with the pruners. Some gardeners find it even more advantageous to use hedge shears, but this type of tool requires more dexterity and it is easy for the inexperienced gardener to make bad or unsightly cuts. Remember, though, that most herbaceous perennial plants recover quickly from pruning mistakes and put forth new, lush foliage within a few weeks time. Don't be afraid to experiment with any of your garden tools to accomplish these pruning tasks.

Pinching must be done early if you wish to retain normal bloom time. Plants that bloom in late spring need to be pinched back early in the spring to not delay their bloom time. Conversely, if you wish to delay a plant's flowering time, it is important to pinch closer to the normal bloom time to get the desired results. However, it is difficult to generalize about the best times for pinching, since there are so many factors involved. Seasonal weather, soil fertility, plant species and individual objectives are some of the factors that affect pinching practices. As a general rule, most pinching is done in May or before the middle of June. But this is not set in stone and it is important to experiment in your own garden zone and ecosystem to learn what works best for you.

Chrysanthemums are the first plants that come to mind when the subject of pinching arises. Almost every gardener has pinched back mums at one time or another. Mums' dense, multi-branched growth habits make them ideal candidates for pinching to delay flower time, increase the number or size of blossoms, or to control height. The usual technique is to pinch lower growing species twice prior to early July and taller plants up to three or four times. Some new varieties of mums are more naturally shaped in their overall growth habits and may not require pinching at all. Be careful when pinching or cutting back or you could end up with a garden full of rounded plants. Unless you are emulating the formal, controlled look that expert Japanese gardeners have perfected over the years, it is usually more attractive to maintain a natural look in perennial gardens.

Individual plants can be pinched back in stages to avoid large holes in the garden. Pinch only one half of a plant and then wait for the new growth to occur before pinching the other half of the plant. Also, pinching is a main means for staggering the bloom time of plants in a group. In mass plantings, try pinching back the plants on the outer edges and leave the inner ones untouched. This will result in the group as a whole blooming for a longer period of time. Staggered bloom is not as dramatic as when an entire group blooms in mass, but it prolongs bloom time by weeks and can add valuable color to otherwise flower-devoid summer gardens.

> To quote an old adage: "Don't pinch after the 4th of July if you would like plants to re-bloom before frost."

CUTTING BACK

Cutting back differs from pinching primarily in the amount of plant material removed and tools used. Cutting back involves removal of from two inches up to a foot or more of foliage. It often saves time because it is usually only done once, while pinching is done in a series of two or more sessions. Cutting back mainly focuses on foliage, usually a significant amount as well as the removal of spent flower heads (deadheads). It is a regenerative means of encouraging a flush of new growth and/or flowers, but it can also control height and time of flowering. This method of pruning is very species-specific, and it is not totally clear why certain species of plants react differently than others to this type of pruning.

Reasons to Cut Back

Some plants are cut back to remove deteriorating vegetative growth, as in some silver-leaved artemisia species in which flowering sometimes causes an overall loss of vigor. Once cut back, these plants put forth new, healthy growth, which results in less stressed plants, which in turn are less prone to disease, insects and weather.

Young plants directly from their nursery containers often are leggy and will get a better start if they are cut back at planting time. This promotes branching and directs more energy toward root development. Try not to be too timid about this initial cutting back because this type of plant really benefits from an early cutting back.

Cutting back results in bushy, strong plants since it promotes branching just as the previous types of pruning discussed in this chapter. When used on plants grown primarily for their foliage, it is similar to shearing. Old, worn-out hedge plants such as yew and boxwood can be cut back almost to the ground in early spring for total rejuvenation. Cutting back usually leads to a more vigorous plant, and even a longer life in certain species. Examples of cutting back carried out in an extreme manner are the pollarded, English landscape trees whose massive trunks are topped by stubby branches.

A strong cutting-back before flowering usually limit a plant's height. The sedum, S. 'Autumn Joy', benefits from being cut back by one-half in early June. When it blooms in late summer, it will be shorter and more compact and less prone to falling open from the center.

In windy sites, cutting back is a useful practice for protecting plants that might suffer damage from strong winds. Also, less staking is required if tall perennials are cut back early in the growing season.

Cutting back is usually the second step of a two-step pruning process. Many perennial plants are deadheaded early in the growing season and later on cut back to their basal foliage to encourage a second bloom. Plants cut back to their basal leaves often grow new foliage and re-bloom faster than plants which were only partially cut back.

Cutting back certain species of plants early in the growing season extends bloom time, and interest in the garden. The later blossoms will be smaller but they are usually more numerous, and if the plants are cut back at the proper time, they can be timed to bloom in conjunction with others nearby. Gardeners should make these pruning decisions relative to their artistic goals. Every year, a new look can be created in the same garden using identical plants by simply cutting back differently from year to year.

Gardeners who choose to cut back only once a season can greatly simplify their maintenance chores. A great time to cut back is when spring flowering shrubs have just finished blooming and are ready for their annual pruning. For gardeners on tight schedules, carrying out these two pruning chores at the same time is more efficient. When choosing pruning plans, take into account family activities such as vacations and amount of leisure time spent together. Try to fit pruning chores into your timetable, not vice versa. You will do a better job if you have time to do the chore properly.

Timing and Techniques

A general rule to follow is that the more plant material that is cut back or the closer it is pruned to its normal date of flowering, the greater the delay in flowering. If you wish no delay in flowering and no decrease in bloom size, cut back prior to June. However, a plant cut back on a certain date will not necessarily have its flowering delayed by 15 days longer than another plant which was cut back 15 days later than the first one. This is not an exact science and it is important to remember that factors such as the age of a plant and its overall vigor, along with the local weather for the season all play parts in the timing of the delayed bloom period.

Gardeners can often determine the type of cutting back required by individual plants by simply observing their structures after flowering. It is usually obvious which plants should be cut back all the way back to their basal leaves or to two inches from the ground, because these plants usually exhibit tall stems that are mostly devoid of leaves or branching. Other plants, such as coreopsis, look best cut back to six inches above the ground.

Stressed summer plants which have gotten very leggy or attacked by pests or disease can be completely rejuvenated by a harsh cut-back all the way to the ground or to basal leaves. Follow this type of pruning with a thorough watering, soil aeration and a dose of liquid fertilizer such as fish emulsion or other quick-acting organic fertilizer to give plants an extra boost. If they don't come back this season, they will be back the next season for sure.

The age of a plant affects how and when it should be cut back. First-year plants are usually vigorous and may flower throughout the season with no cutting back required. As a plant becomes more mature, it often demands more cutting back depending upon its species. Also, hot, dry spells cause a high level of stress and a strong cut-back at any point usually rejuvenates plants and stimulates strong bursts of new growth.

Be aware of a plant's natural growth habits because some plants, such as goldenrod, can develop very odd shapes if pruned too late in the growing season. Unless you are striving for a bit of the Dr. Seuss look in your gardens, it is best to learn when it is too late to cut back certain plants. Remember that experience teaches, so even timid gardeners should jump in and try this type of pruning. For the first few years, practice on plants that are expendable or easily replaced, until you begin to learn how individual plants respond.

Short-lived perennial or biennial species can have their lives prolonged by several years if cut back immediately after flowering and before seeds set. Hollyhock and foxglove are two examples of this type of plant. Be careful to cut no lower than two inches above the ground to avoid damaging new, emerging buds.

Certain woody perennials, such as artemisia, lavender, santolina and thyme benefit from being cut back to four-six inches in early to mid-summer as they start to die back and become leggy. Don't be afraid to do this cutting back because within a few weeks these plants will branch and fill out with fresh foliage to brighten the summer garden.

Plants such as aster and Joe-Pye weed can be cut back to create a more pleasing shape and to stagger bloom time. Tall asters look better if their outer stems are pinched back early in the season in order to hide the leafless, lower legs of the untouched inner stalks. Clumps of Joe-Pye weed can also be enhanced by pinching back some stems and not others, to create less uniform, more natural plants. Keep in mind that if you do this one-time cut-back later than mid-June, the flowers may be delayed until very late summer or even into early fall. If you live in a more northern garden zone, these long awaited flowers may arrive at the same time as an early frost.

Geranium (cranesbill) includes a wide variety of low-growing species which are among the prettiest and most aromatic of all the summer ground covers. The blossoms are spectacular in the early spring, but as the summer progresses some of them get tatty and unsightly. They can be pruned in a number of ways depending upon the variety and their condition at the time, as well as individual

pruning preferences. Some gardeners cut all the stems back to the basal leaves, while others pull out entire stems (which thins and opens up the matted plant material). In other cases, it may only be necessary to deadhead or deadleaf. In any case, cranesbill always comes back with a fresh new look, and often re-blooms if some type of summer pruning has been done.

When Russian sage reaches 12 inches in height, it is advantageous to pinch or cut it back to one-half its height. These plants tend to become tall and ungainly if left to their own devises. A simple pruning early in the growing season encourages them to branch instead of flop all over their neighboring plants as the season progresses.

The practiced gardener waters just enough,
but never too much!

AUGUST

Watering Techniques, Practices, and Systems

ugust at Muddy Creek is inevitably hot, humid and buggy. And while I often seek relief in the shade, our plants have no such refuge. However, I do gain some comfort knowing that plants have their own means of escape. Nature has blessed them with the ability to enter a state of arrest. During periods of drought, plants close their leaf pores to protect themselves from fatal water deprivation. This important survival tactic will be discussed in greater detail within this chapter.

My August chores at Muddy Creek consist of deadheading and making sure the gardens receive enough water to remain healthy. When our gardens were first planted, a local irrigation company installed an automatic, state-of-the-art watering system. One summer I yanked most of it from the garden beds. I had come to the realization that my nature is much better served by the old-fashioned method of watering with hoses. Admittedly, there are days when these cantankerous hoses seem to get the better of me. And for brief moments I envy my friend Robin, whose devoted husband follows along behind her unraveling those unruly beasts. But, on sweltering summer days, as I pause to drench my overheated body with my hose, I am reminded of why I am so ill-suited for modern garden technology. The child in me has refused to leave.

The material introduced in this chapter should prove helpful in determining which type of watering system best suits your personal temperament and gardening needs. Hopefully, it will help you avoid wasting time and money on the wrong system. But most of all, I hope it will encourage you to conserve and use water responsibly. The future of our planet may depend upon it!

FACTORS THAT INFLUENCE
WATER REQUIREMENTS

Climate. This book is primarily concerned with perennial gardens located in areas which experience a winter season or period of dormancy. Watering chores in these growing regions are conducted only when deemed necessary, rather than on a daily basis. For example, gardens in the northwestern states of Washington and Oregon require far less supplemental water than gardens located in the Mid-Atlantic region of the United States.

Weather. The average weather year after year determines local climates. Certain years can bring highly unusual, out of the ordinary weather, especially with the recent phenomenon of global warming. Long periods of extra hot, dry spells or cold, rainy stretches can devastate a normally healthy garden. Even within a single growing season, supplemental water needs can vary immensely, and occasional water shortages can occur almost anywhere.

Soil Type. The type of soil in a garden greatly affects how much supplemental water is needed each growing season. As discussed in the March chapter, sandy soils allow water to pass through with sieve-like speed, while heavy clay soils tend to retain water and are often saturated for long periods of time. So, pay strict attention to your soil type and even to soil variations within individual garden beds. Always keep in mind the long-range goal of improving poor soils by regular

additions of soil amendments, such as compost. However, all gardens are bound to have a few ongoing problem areas. Whenever any trouble spots occur, you should adjust your watering techniques accordingly.

Location. As a rule, gardens located in the shade require less water than those growing in full sun. However, be aware that shade trees suffering from drought may greedily soak up most of the available water. Birch trees are famous for leaving very little water for underlying plants. Or, the reverse can happen where underlying plants take more than their share of water. So just be aware that it is sometimes tricky to supply the correct amount of water for both a tree and its underplantings.

Genetic Disposition. Almost all plants need a consistent supply of water to grow and remain healthy. Plants are comprised of 90% water and are the lifeblood of our planet. However, plants vary greatly in their individual requirements for water. Cacti are genetically constructed to survive in hot, dry conditions. Their leaves, stems and roots are designed to act as reservoirs for storing water, while their waxy and often spike-like leaves limit the amount of water loss. At the opposite end of the spectrum are bog plants, which need to have their roots perpetually wet in order to survive. However, most perennial plants lie somewhere in between these two extremes. Thus, I can't stress enough the importance of understanding the genetic makeup of a plant before placing it in your garden. Not only does the plant's survival depend upon it, but much water and labor can be saved if care is taken to make sure each plant is given a home that best suits its growing needs.

DETERMINING SUPPLEMENTAL WATER NEEDS

Plants take up water, nutrients and oxygen primarily through their root systems. However, as plants open their pores (stomata) in their leaves to take in carbon dioxide for photosynthesis, they allow water to escape into the air. This process of water loss in plants is called transpiration and many botanists refer to this process as the motor of plant life. During the growing season, this constant exchange of water from plant root systems up through their stems and out into the surrounding air is more efficient than any man-made motor.

At the same time transpiration is going on in plants, the soil is constantly losing moisture through the process of evaporation. Hot, dry or windy weather greatly increases the rate of soil evaporation, while cool, overcast conditions slow it down. These two processes of water loss in gardens — transpiration in plants and evaporation from the soil — are referred to as evapotranspiration when considered together. Attempting to scientifically calculate water losses should be left to serious botanists, but the amateur gardener can benefit greatly by understanding these basic principles of water loss.

Home gardeners can simplify the process of determining their garden's water needs by following the one inch per week rule. This method entails measuring rainfall each time it occurs during the active growing season. If less than an inch has fallen in a week, supplemental watering should be done to bring the total up to an inch. Except in extreme weather situations, such as extended droughts, this should satisfy the water requirements for most perennials. Please note that dew does not add to the net water gain of plants, but it does cool them before the heat of the day.

The least expensive measuring system consists of placing metal cans, preferably with straight, vertical sides, in various locations throughout your garden beds. After each rainfall, use a metal ruler to measure and record the depth of water in each can. The can with the least amount of water should be the determining measure to ensure that the entire garden receives adequate amounts of water. If you would like to take a more scientific approach, rain gauges can be bought at garden centers, by mail

order or online. They are more expensive than using leftover food cans, but they are easier to read and monitor over the long run.

Regardless of which type of rain gauge you choose, be sure to conduct an overhead sprinkler test prior to your first supplemental watering. Do this test by running the sprinkler with the faucet fully open. After one hour, measure your cans or gauges to see how much water your sprinkler delivered in that time. The results will serve as a general guideline for future watering.

FREQUENCY AND TIMING OF SUPPLEMENTAL WATERING

New perennial beds require shallow and more frequent watering than older, established beds. New plants have shallow, fragile root systems which can easily become stressed in high heat or drought situations. It is smart garden practice to check new beds or plants every other day for an entire month after planting to guard against excessive moisture loss. Be on the lookout for flagging plants and probe the soil a few inches below the surface to see if it is moist.

After the first crucial month, new plants can be treated in the same manner as established plants. Less-frequent, longer watering sessions encourage roots to grow deeper which gives better protection from heat and drought. But, it is wise to continue to monitor the water needs of first-year plants throughout the entire growing season.

Do not tend your plants to death!

Perennial beds with deep, well-established root systems are fairly resistant to dry, hot conditions. Many gardeners err on the side of the "more is better" theory when it comes to watering practices. I would like to reiterate once again that most of the rot diseases caused by fungi occur when gardens are kept on the wet side. So, to keep your plants more resistant to disease, try to avoid the pitfall of over-watering.

A good test for determining if a plant has been over-watered is to observe it in the cool of the evening. If it does not come out of its daytime wilt, then stop watering! It more than likely has been given too much water and is suffering from oxygen deprivation. Often, simply providing some daytime shade for a new plant is more beneficial than watering. If the soil feels moist three to four inches deep around the struggling plant and it is still experiencing wilt, try shielding it with a shade screen during the heat of the day. Remember, it is always best to base decisions on thoughtful observation and not from knee-jerk reactions.

Long, dry summers may require watering well into the fall season. Remember that plants continue to actively grow roots right up until they enter the winter (dormant) season. Many gardeners forget about watering late in the growing season and don't realize how important it is to continue to pay attention at this time of year. New plants especially, but old plants as well, should not go into the winter deficient in moisture.

Evergreens, in particular, are vulnerable to desiccation (foliage dry-out) since they retain their leaves and continue to transpire throughout the dormant period. Winter death in evergreens occurs more often from water loss than as a result of frozen roots.

It is equally important to avoid heavy over-watering just prior to freezing. A plant's hardiness can be affected if it is given too much water just prior to winter, particularly if it has been in a stressed state. It is almost impossible to over-emphasize the importance of watering properly throughout the entire growing season. Sound watering practices will greatly enhance your plants' chance of survival through the long winter season!

MANUAL AND MECHANICAL WATERING METHODS

Spray Attachments and Watering Cans

Determining the best method to water your garden is somewhat dependent upon its size. A small, city garden may be best served using a short hose with a dispersal spray attachment or even a hand-held watering can. Hose-end watering tools soften the force of the spray and disperse the water evenly. They are also excellent devices for delivering water directly to the root ball without wetting foliage. This is a big advantage because wet foliage often causes fungal diseases in susceptible plants. On the other hand, if any plants are infested with aphids or spider mites, you should wash them off with a strong blast from a hose.

Watering by hand is often more beneficial from an ecological standpoint because water is delivered only to plants in need of supplemental water. Hand watering also provides the chance to experience one of life's simplest pleasures. There are few things as rewarding as watering my gardens on a summer morning before my fellow humans are up and about. These peaceful and restorative moments, when time seems to stand still, give me the energy to face the demanding world outside Muddy Creek.

Overhead Sprinklers

Most overhead sprinklers attach to the end of hoses and come in a variety of styles and types. Trial and error is probably the most effective way to learn which type best suits your needs. Watering with hoses entails dragging hoses to all parts of your garden and making sure they are shut off or moved elsewhere when the proper amount of water has been delivered. This method can really try your patience since hoses seem to have a mind of their own and tend to kink or snag. Also, hose-end attachments can be tricky to adjust, so it is important to choose the type that you can operate easily and can count on. All of us at one time or another have gone out to check on a hose-end sprinkler, only to find it uprooted and trying to dig a hole to Middle-earth.

Two main benefits of using overhead sprinklers are that they are cheaper and easier to implement than drip methods. Most gardeners already own several hoses and the spray attachments are inexpensive to purchase. They deliver water in a similar fashion to rainfall and they can be adjusted in a number of ways, such as the distance covered and degrees of rotation. Aphid or spider mite infestations may be partially washed away in the process, but usually they need an extra spray from a hose to loosen them from their hiding places on the underside of leaves and inside buds.

If possible, water plants early in the morning. This allows plants ample time to dry off before evening and cuts down considerably on the amount of water lost through evaporation, since it is cooler and often less windy at this time of day. During dry periods, this type of watering offers the added benefit of cleaning the dust off leaves and cooling plants before they face the heat of the day.

Overhead sprinklers need to be turned on and off manually by the gardener. To avoid forgetting to move them or shut them off, it is wise to set a small kitchen

timer or keep a note pad in a very visible spot in the house as a reminder. Another option is to purchase a timer that fits between the hose and the faucet which can be set to automatically shut off the water.

DRIP IRRIGATION SYSTEMS

Removable Piping

This type of watering consists of laying pipes, usually made of plastic, throughout your garden beds. Tiny holes, called emitters, are spaced at frequent intervals along the piping and serve to disperse water slowly and evenly into the soil. When purchasing these pipes, be aware that the emitters are available in several different application and pressure rates. For instance, hoses with pressure-compensating emitters will ensure that water is distributed evenly throughout the piping, even as the ground levels change. It is important to know your soil type before buying drip hoses, to ensure that you purchase the type most suitable for your garden soils.

Drip hoses force water to radiate horizontally, as well as directly downward, which ensures an even distribution of water throughout entire garden beds. Water is distributed about three times slower than with over-head systems which allows more time for soil absorption, and therefore less water is wasted from runoff. Drip hoses are highly efficient and environmentally responsible because they send water directly to the root balls where it is needed most. And, they offer the major benefit of keeping water away from vulnerable foliage which contributes to healthier gardens.

Drip hoses should run for several hours to thoroughly soak beds to a depth of three to four inches. When first using your drip irrigation hoses, dig around the entire bed after a set period of watering (usually one hour). This will tell you how wide and deep the water has penetrated and will allow you to make the proper timing adjustments for future watering.

Drip hoses are either buried a few inches deep or laid directly on the soil surface and covered with a few inches of compost and/or mulch. Whichever method you choose, it is important to keep the piping close to the surface in order to monitor it. The biggest negative to the use of temporary drip pipes is the installation time required at the beginning of the season, as well as the removal time in the fall. If you neglect to remove them from the gardens in the fall they might suffer damage from frozen soil or be damaged by small animals when food supplies are low.

Another drawback to this method of watering is that certain types of insects flourish more easily when there is less overhead waterfall to rinse them off. So it is even more important to police your gardens for pest infestations if you choose this method of watering. Also, it is very easy to damage these hidden drip pipes with a spade or fork, and you might not detect any leaks until a quagmire has developed. Regular observation is essential with this type of system in order to detect problems early before any serious plant loss has occurred. And always make sure you have plenty of patching kits on hand. These kits are quick and easy to use and will allow you to fix leaks immediately. Drip hoses are fairly short-lived and often last only four to five years, mainly as a result of clogging from chemical deposits contained in water. However, if your water is conditioned, there may not be an excessive buildup of minerals in the piping.

Automated Watering Systems

Automatic systems come in both drip and overhead watering modes and are best purchased through local companies who specialize in their sale and installation. Before choosing this type of watering method, understand how your system operates and take an active part in the planning process. Some systems have such complex, computerized control centers that it takes a rocket scientist to operate them. This was my downfall and one of the main reasons I removed most of this high-tech piping from my garden beds last summer.

These systems consist of very stiff, synthetic piping that is laid just under the surface of the soil in the same manner that temporary piping is laid. It weaves its way throughout entire beds and disperses water by either overhead sprinkling or by the drip method. Even though they are pre-programmed, they should still be monitored on a weekly basis. During periods of extended rainfall, the delivery amounts may need to be decreased or even stopped, while in severe droughts it may become necessary to increase the water amounts. Some high-tech systems actually have built-in rain gauges or moisture sensors that eliminate the need for such close monitoring. These gauges need to be checked and cleaned on a regular basis to keep them functioning properly.

One of the biggest advantages to automated watering systems is that they eliminate the chore of day-to-day water monitoring. They can save a tremendous amount of time over the course of a gardening season. They also allow gardeners the freedom to take vacations, even during the dry summer season. But, make sure you spend enough time learning about the operation and maintenance of an automatic system before you make the decision to purchase one. They can really add to garden costs if you are continually calling the installation company to your property every time a leak or clog occurs or the computer is on the blink.

Another disadvantage to this system is that the extensive network of underground piping can get in the way while cultivating your beds. These pipes are usually installed fairly close together (12 to 18 inches apart), which can make managing the soil a hazardous proposition. Before a shovel or fork can be plunged into the soil, it is necessary to locate the tubing to avoid piercing a pipe or valve in the process. Also, it can be difficult to move or divide older plants if their root systems have become entwined in the piping. Last summer, as I felt more and more hemmed in by this tight network of piping, I delighted in removing some of it from my garden beds. It was simply too restrictive for my personal garden habits and was a constant thorn in my side.

So, put a lot of thought into this type of watering system before choosing it for your gardens. Automated systems are expensive to purchase and install and can be a huge waste of money if they turn out to be the wrong choice for your gardens. I learned the hard way. I hope all of you will profit from my experience.

"Of all the rain that falls
on a densely planted English garden,
two-thirds is promptly re-circulated by the plants.
(Only one-third drains away into the ground.)
A large shade tree can draw three to four gallons
of water a day from the soil and move it
into the atmosphere.

— *PRINCIPLES OF GARDENING*, HUGH JOHNSON

The whole of a garden rests on a compost heap,
as telling as an archeological dig!

— Anna Pavord

SEPTEMBER

Home Composting

I n milder regions of the United States, gardeners spend September scurrying about taking advantage of plant sales. But here in Vermont, I've learned that early frosts can do permanent damage by pushing newly rooted, small perennial plants out of the ground. So I work hard to squelch late summer buying urges, which affords me the extra time to amend and clean garden beds and to provide winter protection for vulnerable plants. But I'll defer my discussions of these important fall chores until next month in order to spend September singing the praises of home composting.

My first introduction to home composting was 10 years ago when I married my husband Terry. I entered our marriage with three cats, a dog and a chainsaw, but Terry brought along 5,000 worms. Terry had been worm farming in his basement for a number of years and was not about to abandon his old friends. Watching Terry tend his brood each week was a terrific learning experience and laid the groundwork for my future composting efforts. And even though I now create copious amounts of compost outdoors, those worms still produce the richest compost at Muddy Creek.

Hopefully this chapter will inspire those of you who are not already tuned into the wonders of composting. It is one of the oldest garden practices in the world and can be carried out in the smallest of gardens. Simply put, compost is decayed organic matter that conditions and feeds the soil. This chapter lays out very specific methods and techniques for producing compost correctly and efficiently. However, all that is really required is to set aside a spot to stack your organic waste materials until they break down enough to spread on your gardens. The important thing is to choose a method that suits your lifestyle and join in on the fun!

COMPOSTING — AS OLD AS LIFE ITSELF

Composting is the oldest form of soil amending in the world. Nature has been creating compost since primitive plant life first evolved. In conjunction with water and air, it is one of the main reasons life is able to perpetuate itself. As plants grow, they deplete soil of nutrients and the soil becomes less porous. In nature, natural cycles of life and death rejuvenate the soil.

Beginning thousands of years ago, early cultivators began to imitate the cycles of life and death that they observed in nature. Leaves decomposing in the forest and vegetation sprouting from dung piles were among nature's first indicators of the rejuvenating benefits of decaying organic matter. Through trial and error, early farmers learned to compost a wide variety of natural materials, such as wood ash, straw, dead fish, corn stalks, blood from animal sacrifices, and crushed bones. As civilizations advanced, people everywhere began to spread manure on fields and to recycle most of their organic waste into compost heaps on the edges of their villages.

Amazingly, the basic concept of composting has remained unchanged over the thousands of years since humans first discovered its values. Even in this advanced world filled with sophisticated technology, the practice of amending soil with compost continues to reign supreme over use of synthetic products. And today, as modern civilizations increasingly deplete the world's resources, there is an urgent need to conserve what's left of our energy supplies. Each year, 2% of the natural gas in the United States is used to manufacture chemical fertilizers. If each of us were to adopt the practice of home composting or send our refuse to community recycling centers, we could make a significant difference in this energy drain. My hope is that this chapter will inspire and guide those of you who have yet to learn the virtues of this age-old, life-sustaining practice.

WHAT HAPPENS IN A COMPOST PILE

Decomposition occurs largely as a result of a succession of organisms that specialize in feeding upon dead or dying organic matter and actually change the chemistry of this matter as they break it down. In return, the organic matter supplies these decomposing organisms with food and energy to carry out their life cycles of growth and reproduction. This frenzied feeding activity is a physiological form of oxidation (biological burning) — it's why a compost pile heats up or "cooks."

Bacteria and fungi are the two main types of microorganisms that do the lion's share of the work in this complex food chain. Each of these microscopic organisms carries out its duties in different ways and at different stages during the decomposition process.

Many larger animal forms also take part in the decomposition of a compost pile. They are referred to as physical decomposers because they break down the matter by biting, grinding and chewing. Earthworms are the stars among this army of larger decomposing agents. Most fertile soil has at one time or another passed through the bodies of earthworms. These priceless creatures spend their entire lives oxygenating and enriching soil. Working in the final, more stable stages of the decay process, their castings (manure excretions) contain balanced, easily absorbable plant nutrients, as well as plentiful amounts of beneficial bacteria. This worm manure is among the highest quality humus found on earth! (Humus is organic matter in its final stage of decomposition.) Flies are also beneficial to a compost pile and they often spend their larval stages in the pile, emerging in the spring to feast. They also provide aerial transportation for beneficial bacteria which attach to their bodies for a free ride to the pile.

Ants join in on the fun by providing the valuable service of moving raw materials from one place to another. The damp bounty of a compost pile is a huge attraction for slugs and snails, and is a far better place for them to be dining than in the hosta beds. Many other bugs and insects take part in the decomposition of a compost pile—spiders, mites, centipedes and nematodes, to name just a few.

The vast number and types of decomposing agents at work in a compost pile all serve to keep each other in balance. As decomposing organisms die off or become inactive at various stages in the compost pile, they serve as food for the decomposers that follow them. This complex, perfectly engineered process of decay is one of the miracles of our natural world. Each group paves the way for the next crew of decomposing organisms until all of the material is broken down into nutrient-rich, easily absorbable humus. Chemical fertilizers, quite simply, are a poor substitute for this superb product of nature.

NUTRIENTS NEEDED TO SUPPORT
LIFE IN A COMPOST PILE

The decomposing organisms at work in a compost pile need carbon, nitrogen, phosphorous and potassium, as well as lesser amounts of the minor elements, in order to thrive and reproduce. They are inefficient at performing their tasks unless they are provided the necessary nutrients upon which to feed.

Of these ingredients, carbon and nitrogen are the most vital and they must be present in the proper ratios. Piles containing too much stalky, carbonaceous material (such as leaves) are inefficient and decompose very slowly. On the other hand, piles too high in green (nitrogen-rich) material (such as grass clippings) often putrefy, causing the decomposers to suffocate from lack of oxygen.

MATERIALS AND CONDITIONS
FOR MAKING COMPOST

Carbon Material. Dead vegetation and woody organic matter are the main sources of carbon in a compost pile. Examples of carbon-based materials are dry weeds, leaves, straw, sawdust, newspaper, corn stalks and twigs. These materials tend to be dry, coarse and bulky, but once in the compost pile, they can hold 75 to 85% of their weight in moisture.

Nitrogen Materials. Nitrogen is provided from green materials such as fresh-cut grass, food waste, animal by-products and manure of all types. These materials tend to be dense and succulent due to their high moisture content. However, when added to a compost pile, they absorb even more water, often up to 50 to 60% of their body weight. As microorganisms devour these nitrogen-rich materials, they obtain the sustenance necessary for growth and for digesting the tougher, carbon-containing materials.

Soil and Manure. The cheapest and most natural way to introduce microorganisms into a compost pile is to add generous amounts of soil or manure. Both of these ingredients are teeming with beneficial organisms who are always delighted to find themselves in a fresh pile of foodstuff. Also, soil placed throughout a pile keeps down offensive odors, deters flies and helps the pile retain moisture.

Moisture. Soil microbes need enough water to keep them alive, yet if given too much water they drown. Most microorganisms need a minimum moisture content of 12 to 15% in order to become active, and their activity will remain limited until moisture levels reach 45% or higher. *Compost materials should never contain more water than a well wrung-out sponge.*

> A simple rule to follow is to keep moisture levels as high as possible while still allowing pores for air to circulate throughout the pile.

Air. Compost needs air. Along with food and water, oxygen is vital for the existence of the many organisms at work in a pile. If a pile smells or appears slimy, it is probably in a state of putrification. If you think your pile has become saturated, set aside time to restack the pile, adding extra, carbon-based materials to dry it out as you rebuild.

Temperature. Temperature strongly influences the dynamics of a compost pile. Cool outside temperatures slow microbial activity, while the high heat of summer greatly speeds it up. As a pile breaks down, various types of microorganisms are constantly at work at different temperatures. The first decomposing organisms start feeding at temperatures of 50°F or so, and are followed by others who feed in the 112°F to 160°F range. It is crucial to know that a compost heap must reach temperatures as high as 160°F in order to ensure the death of all weed seeds and disease organisms.

So, while a compost pile can be built at any time of the year, nothing much will happen unless the inner parts of a pile are 50°F or higher!

pH. Most decomposers need a pH range of 5.5 to 8.0 to be active. They have a difficult time feeding and digesting materials in a compost pile if the pH is too acidic or alkaline. Composting with a wide range of materials should help keep the pH within an acceptable range.

BUILDING A HOME COMPOST PILE

The methods for building a compost pile are virtually the same whether you create a single, freestanding pile or use elaborate, time-consuming methods. It may take awhile, but it is impossible to fail if all the basic components are present in your pile. Even if you choose the simplest method with virtually no maintenance, your waste will eventually break down into usable compost to spread on your garden.

Any home gardener can build a compost pile by using whatever ingredients are on hand at home, and if needed, from supplemental materials scavenged nearby. It is fairly easy to obtain extra composting materials if you just explore your local area. For instance, one of my daughters works nearby as a woodworker, which means that I have a constant supply of sawdust at my disposal. One woman's waste is another woman's treasure!

Choose an accessible location, preferably in a shady spot! A pile will maintain its moisture levels more easily when not sitting in the direct sun. Also, hot summer sun beating down on a compost heap can kill off decomposers in the pile. Remember that most of these organisms are very temperature sensitive! If your compost is enclosed in a metal container of any sort, it will be even more vulnerable to the summer heat. (More on metal bins at the end of this chapter.) And finally, except in the case of enclosed containers, there should be a similar-sized space right next to this first spot to transfer the compost pile to after it has finished its first stage of decomposition.

Prepare your base by digging and turning the soil 12 inches deep and 3 feet square. Spending the time and labor to expose the soil adds greatly to the drainage, aeration and microbe penetration of the pile.

There are numerous materials to choose from when laying the base of a compost pile. The cheapest and easiest ones include branches, twigs, corn stalks and any other woody materials available to you. Try to keep a pile of woody prunings

on hand just for this purpose. Permanent base materials include cinder blocks and bricks, either of which should be placed on the ground in a manner that will allow air to flow freely through and around them. Whichever material you choose, try not to cut corners by eliminating this base. The pile will decompose much faster if you create a bottom layer that promotes air circulation throughout the pile.

Build the layers as if you were making lasagna, alternating stalky, carbon-rich materials with green, nitrogen-rich materials. *Depending upon the size of your pile and availability of materials, each layer should be two to six inches thick. Try to construct the layers using equal volumes of these two opposing materials; otherwise the ratio of carbon to nitrogen can get out of kilter.* Use as many different raw materials as you can lay your hands on. The greater the variety, the more balanced and richer the finished compost! Also, a wide range of foodstuff attracts a more diverse group of organisms, which in turn ensures a broader range of disease protection. Complete each layer with a one- to two-inch dressing of soil or manure and a liberal sprinkling of water.

Of all the nitrogen-rich, green materials used in composting, manure always takes top prize. Manure is the only natural material besides compost that is a complete food for the soil. Adding liberal amounts to a pile greatly enhances the finished compost. However, manures vary greatly in their composition and nutrient content, depending upon such factors as the animal source and what types of food and bedding were provided to the animals. Be aware that uncomposted manure contains many weed seeds and can be the source of a wide variety of disease organisms. The safest and most efficient way to use manure is to add it to the green layers while building a compost pile. If you insist on using it directly on your garden, make sure it has been aged for at least six months or its richness may kill your plants by burning their roots.

Always keep meat, bones, fat and grease out of a compost pile! These items cause undesirable odors and are an attraction for four-legged pests. Never compost cat, dog or human feces because these materials often harbor disease organisms. Slimy cooked foods should also be avoided as they are slow to decompose, pu-

trefy easily and are magnets for pests. Also, be careful to keep any chemically treated materials out of the compost pile to ensure that your gardens stay free of toxins.

Build the pile about three feet high, making sure that the bottom stays wider than the top to ensure stability. Cover the top of the finished pile with a six-inch layer of soil to hold in moisture. If you have straw on hand, a light layer placed on top at the end will protect the pile from excessive moisture build-up.

Depending upon the weather, it may be necessary to check the pile as often as every few days or so. A simple method of determining water and temperature levels is to stick your hand or a specialized compost thermometer into the pile about a foot. If it feels warm and slightly moist, or registers near or above 160° F, your compost pile is probably decomposing very nicely. After three to six weeks, most well-made compost piles will have cooled down from the initial feeding frenzy.

At this point, it is important to turn the pile to redistribute the materials. Hopefully, you have already prepared a neighboring spot for transferring the pile. Remember to lay rough materials at the bottom of the new pile for continued aeration during this second stage of decomposition. If you lack the room for this two-pile composting method, simply fork the pile onto the ground, rearrange it, and return it to its original spot. Use a long handled pitchfork to transfer the materials into the new pile, making sure the drier, undigested materials are placed in the center and vice versa. Be sure to add water and/or extra green materials if the pile seems too dry. Or add well broken-down carbon-based materials if it seems excessively wet or putrefied.

Maintain this second pile in the same manner as the first, letting it decompose or cool for three to six months, depending upon the weather. It will be ready to use when it is difficult to recognize the originals materials, smells woodsy and is dark and crumbly. Try to use your compost before it decomposes too long. As compost ages, microorganisms continue to feed on its soil aggregates, which results in loss of structure and nutrient depletion.

TECHNIQUES TO SPEED UP
THE COMPOSTING PROCESS

Shred or chop all raw materials before adding them to the pile or bin, making sure that any woody materials are smaller than ¾ inch. Shred all hardwood leaves before using in a compost heap since they take several years to break down on their own. And remember that compost piles decompose most efficiently when the carbon and nitrogen containing materials are present in equal volumes. Keeping these materials in balance will ensure that the carbon/nitrogen ratio is optimal for fast and efficient decomposition.

Turn the pile every three to six days to keep the pile well oxygenated. The new supplies of oxygen introduced by frequent turnings serve as extra fuel for the decomposers madly at work in the pile. Also, by frequently rearranging a compost pile, you can keep a closer eye on its moisture levels. Always add more water or green materials if it is too dry or dry materials if it becomes too wet or waterlogged.

Add plentiful amounts of soil, manure and/or finished compost to a pile as you build it. Each of these materials contains copious amounts of decomposing organisms. These workers will begin to feed immediately upon arrival in the pile, greatly speeding up decomposition.

Buy a specialized compost thermometer (20 inches long with a dial and probe) to monitor the temperature of your pile. This will enable you to more accurately determine if the pile is heating up or cooling down and will dictate the optimal times to turn your pile.

Introduce red worms into the compost during the summer months to further speed things up. Commonly called red wigglers, these specialized worms thrive in compost piles and manure droppings. Capable of surviving higher temperatures than ordinary field worms, they still must wait to be added until the pile is in its cooling down stage. To be sure of your timing, add them only when the interior of your pile is at the same temperature as the outside air, usually three weeks after the last materials have been added to your pile. Red worms can be ordered by mail order or online and should be dropped into holes dug into the pile in groups of 50 to100.

THREE-PILE COMPOSTING METHOD

This is the ultimate and most efficient way to make finished compost, especially if you have large gardens. (I use this method for part of my compost. Since Muddy Creek generates copious amounts of weed material and prunings, we also have huge piles which we turn with our tractor.) The three-pile method allows you the luxury of maintaining piles in various stages of decomposition. Always keep in mind that the proportions of the raw materials used in building any compost pile are more important than the order in which they're layered. The dry woody materials should always be equal in volume to the wet, green materials.

First Pile: This pile contains materials going through the first stages of heating up and cooling down. Move this pile to the second spot when it begins to break down and has a uniform color.

Second Pile: Turn and work this pile until the materials start to look dark and crumbly. This pile will be ready to move to the third spot when it has lots of structure and reached the final stage of decomposition known as humus.

Third Pile: This final pile contains compost in a ready-to-use, finished state. It is best to keep this pile covered with a plastic tarp to prevent loss of nutrients and structure and to avoid weeds seeding into it while it is waiting to be used on your gardens.

METAL OR PLASTIC ENCLOSED COMPOSTING CONTAINERS

Synthetic containers are very limiting in the amounts of compost they can produce, but are often the perfect choice for the small home gardener. They are aesthetically pleasing to look at, hold heat and moisture well and ensure protection from four-legged scavengers. While they cost more than building simple wire or wooden enclosures, you have the advantage of easier turning capability. Be aware, however, that more strength is required to roll a barrel-style container on the ground than is needed to turn a stationary, crankshaft-operated bin. If possible, purchase a bin that is at least one cubic yard in volume. This will enable you to add enough raw materials to build up sufficient mass to obtain the high temperatures required for proper decomposition. These metal or plastic containers can be purchased in a wide variety of sizes and shapes by mail order, online, or from large garden centers.

Compost Tea Recipe

This concoction is teeming with micro-organisms and can be used to boost a plant's natural defenses.

Mix one part mature compost (should contain some manure) with five parts of water in a large bucket. Allow this to brew in the shade for 10 days or so, then filter it through a cheesecloth. Use this mixture half strength to spray on leaves of weakened plants, reapplying every two to three weeks until plant seems robust.

What one gardener finds attractive in the winter garden,
may be an eyesore to another.

OCTOBER

Fall Cleanup

n early October, as daylight wanes and temperatures drop, my outdoor chores center on preparing the gardens for the long Vermont winter. Each year at Muddy Creek, we are blessed with a few days of Indian summer before winter arrives to enshroud us. As I go about cleaning up the gardens, I realize that for me, life does not get any better than this. I am able to satisfy my penchant for order and tidiness while reveling in the lingering warmth and autumn colors that typify October at Muddy Creek.

Below the soil's surface, storage roots are busy receiving energy stores from dying plant material and are stretching out in the still warm soil for a wider hold. It seems as if all the energy of the universe is flowing into the ground at this time of year, where it will rest until reversing its flow upward in the springtime. As I cut, chop, and mulch, I can almost feel this flow of energy. My own habits seem to mimic the plants. I crave comforting teas, nourishing soups, hardy breads, and evenings by our fire.

This month will focus on the first steps of putting a perennial garden to bed for the winter. You will see that there are basic rules to follow, especially in areas with severe winters. I will also discuss the different choices and attitudes surrounding this winter prep work. As always, aesthetics play a large role in my chores here at Muddy Creek. As I discuss these October tasks, you will find that design elements are often in the forefront. I hope this chapter will help to take some of the drudgery out of fall cleanup and add a creative element to your chores.

Northern gardeners spend most of their energy during the fall months cleaning, tidying and readying their gardens for the long winter season. The most important of these tasks involves cutting or chopping back many herbaceous perennials, digging out a few remaining weeds and adding water to any soils deficient in moisture.

Gardeners vary in how they approach these fall chores. Some customize these tasks to suit their lifestyles and personal garden aesthetics. It used to be common garden practice to totally cut back all stems and foliage to near ground level. Beds were often left looking desolate, especially those devoid of any evergreens, woody shrubs or trees. During the dormant season, these naked beds showed little signs of life.

Fortunately, attitudes changed in recent years. The gardening world has developed a new awareness and appreciation of the faded beauty of certain herbaceous plants left standing. There has also been a renewed sensitivity to the winter needs of birds, butterflies and other creatures beneficial to our environment. At Muddy Creek, I take the more naturalistic approach. The following pages focus on how to add more beauty to your gardens in wintertime without compromising the health of your plants in the process.

REASONS TO REMOVE DEAD PLANT MATERIAL

The most important reason to remove vegetative debris from gardens in the fall is to avoid harboring pests and diseases that can winter-over in some life form in these remains. Always remove wet, mushy debris, because undesirable fungi and bacteria are particularly happy in that type of environment. Be sure to take away all fallen deadheads and excess leaves because they also provide shelter for these undesirables.

Heavily matted leaves do not break down easily and tend to create moist, slimy mats under which fungal diseases, such as crown rot, thrive. It is best to shred leaves with a mower or shredder before adding them to your compost pile. It is well worth your time to make a separate compost from the leaves off your trees. The leaves from most trees contain twice the mineral content of manure. *Since dried leaves are lacking in nitrogen content, add layers of manure (alfalfa meal or bone meal work almost as well) into the leaf compost as you build your piles. A mixture of five parts leaves to one part manure is a perfect ratio for accelerating the decomposition process of leaves.*

Cutting back many perennials to a height of four to six inches is considered good garden practice. This removes the seedpods and most of the stems and leaves, but allows the remaining stubble to provide a bit of shelter and insulation to the crowns. Welcome snow will settle in and around these short stalks, laying down a nature-made winter blanket.

Many perennials, if left uncut, can be major eyesores in the winter garden. Tall-stemmed plants such as asters tend to blacken if left standing, and the leaves of certain types of cranesbill (geranium) turn an ugly black after a hard frost. And, while many perennial grasses possess strong stems and fare beautifully throughout the winter, some of them become distractions as they fall over, break or lose their color.

Perennial plants which are slow to awaken and emerge from the soil in the spring should always be left with four to six inches of standing stems. These short, remaining stems will act as markers and help to keep these tardy plants from being disturbed when carrying out spring chores. I sometimes go one step further and place a wooden stake near a plant for further identification, especially if it is new to my garden.

Certain gardens look best neat and tidy for the winter months. For formal gardens, common practice calls for removing most of the herbaceous perennial debris. This style of garden provides plenty of winter beauty from structural elements such as trimmed hedges and shrubs, walls, statuary, parterres, pergolas and numerous other architectural features. On the other hand, naturalistic gardens like mine at Muddy Creek look best when winter beds are left with plenty of foliage and seed heads. The subtle beauty of these standing remnants provides a natural transition from the gardens into the meadows, woods and farm fields beyond.

Another reason to carry out a more thorough cleanup in the fall is to gain a head start on springtime garden chores. Most gardeners lead busy lives and it helps to be efficient with our leisure hours. Garden debris is often easier to remove in the fall when the remains are crisp and easy to cut. In the spring, vegetative remains can be tough and soggy from absorbing winter moisture and spring rainfall. If time allows, remove any weeds left over from summer. Well-tended perennial beds are loose and easy to work with at this time of year, and the more weeds removed in the fall, the less seed set for the next season. The following spring, chores can be jumped into without leftover debris obstructing your work.

THE OTHER SIDE OF THE COIN

Winter interest is not just provided by evergreens (including ground covers), rocks, stone walls, arbors, woody shrubs or trees. While all of these elements create the essence of winter gardens, there is another layer of interest to consider. By choosing appropriate perennials to leave standing, an entire vegetative under-story with interesting textures and subtle tones can be enjoyed during the dormant season. Plants as coneflowers, blackberry lily, sunflowers and a multitude of grasses serve to brighten our spirits on drab, winter days.

Herbaceous perennials left uncut provide vital winter food and sanctuary to birds, and to butterflies and other favorable bugs. The protective leaves and stems of uncut vegetation are safe havens for butterflies to lay eggs and to pupate. If we cut all these plants back to ground level, we may well be eliminating our next season's crop of butterflies. Also, as winter birds dart back and forth scavenging for food, they need to seek shelter amongst vegetative remains to rest and evade predators.

Many perennials have mound-like, evergreen crowns, which besides providing protection, create winter interest as they poke their green, textural forms out of the snow. Walking along my garden paths on wintry days, my spirits always brighten when I glimpse the muted halos of thyme, ginger, wintergreen, paxistima, donkey spurge, and hellebores asleep in their snowy nests.

There are certain perennials I chose to leave untouched strictly for the beauty they offer on icy winter mornings. Frozen families of grasses, sunflower stalks with snow-capped bonnets, fences festooned with frosted seed-heads and snow-garlanded evergreens invite me to rush out and play as if a winter carnival had just arrived.

HOW AND WHEN TO PRUNE AND CUT BACK

Hand pruners or hedge shears are the best tools for cutting back dead plant material. Power tools are inappropriate in most instances, because it is important to go slowly in order to see what you are doing. If I am unable to cut through some of the tougher grasses, Terry comes out with his hatchet and chops them back in no time at all. Take care when raking up your cuttings, because it is easy to uproot perennials which are shallow rooted or newly planted. Don't forget to bag or burn any diseased material to keep from contaminating your compost heap.

Cut down all plants you know will become eyesores or provide shelter for undesirable pests in the winter garden. These should include all plants that become slimy piles of mush as soon as they experience a hard frost, such as hostas and Solomon's seal. Also, plants such as daylilies and tall campanulas should go, as they offer little beauty and are distractions to the eye. If you are unsure about

cutting certain plants back, wait until November or December to determine which should go or stay.

The ideal time to cut back herbaceous plants is just after the first killing frost in the fall, when you are sure the plants have gone completely dormant. If plants are still actively growing, this cutting back might stimulate tender, new growth which can be damaged by frigid temperatures. Also, plants at this time of year are busy conserving their energy stores for the following season. Their very survival may be compromised if they are stimulated to use these reserves at the wrong time.

Woody plants that retain some of their leaves, such as lavender, thyme, and heather, should be left uncut in the fall. These plants should never be cut all the way to the ground, because they set buds on their woody stems rather than in their crowns or below soil level. Also, uncut woody stems and foliage material provide vital insulation for half-hardy plants. In areas with severe winters, further protection can be provided by mulching with pine boughs, straw or other appropriate material. (This will be discussed in depth in November). In late spring cut away any parts damaged by winterkill and cut the plant back to healthy wood and/or to the first set of strong buds. This is also a good time to rejuvenate older, straggly plants by severely chopping them back.

Short-lived perennials such as foxglove and mullein should have their stems cut back to their basal leaves. Shake dried seed heads in the vicinity of the parent plant in order to encourage new seedlings for the next season. Another approach is to bend over a stem until the seed head rests on the ground, and then pin it down with a drip hose staple or a bent piece of wire. Pinning down seed heads in this way marks the spot where the seedlings will germinate, lessening their chances of mistakenly being weeded out of the garden in the springtime.

Always leave fronds on marginally hardy ferns until springtime to help protect their crowns and buds. Once spring arrives, it is easy to cut and rake up this dead material. Buddleia's woody stems are also best left uncut until spring. Their stems should then be cut back to six inches or so from the ground, preferably just above the first set of strong buds. In northern regions, harsh winter weather causes these half-hardy, woody perennials to die back and act as if they were herbaceous. I have to cut mine almost to ground level each spring in order to find strong, healthy buds.

Each plant has a regime it will
ultimately insist upon.

NOVEMBER

Protective Measures for Winter

n November, garden chores center around preparing for the dormant season. There is much scurrying about gathering in ceramic pots, moving vulnerable sculpture, and placing protective covering over half-hardy plants. I always love the ethereal aura of the boxwood garden after Terry and I have wrapped each shrub in burlap. It looks like a family of miniature monks all settled in for a winter of meditation.

Adaptation is the key to longevity. Plants have managed to survive over the centuries because of their ability to change. In colder regions, hardy plants have geared themselves to do most of their growing while soils are warm and wet. But even more importantly, they have programmed themselves to shut down operations and go dormant as soils freeze. Deciduous shrubs and trees drop their leaves, while evergreens slow their metabolisms and go into partial hibernation. And for the most part, plants do quite well if they are grown in their proper hardiness zones. It is mainly when gardeners meddle with these parameters that extra precautions need to be taken. For gardeners such as me, who are on the cusp between two hardiness zones — zones 4 and 5 — there is a continual temptation to grow plants that are better suited for warmer climates.

This chapter defines hardiness zones and explains how plants protect themselves in order to survive the dormant season. The discussions center around what determines plant hardiness and how gardeners can use that information to their best advantage.

PLANT HARDINESS

Plants designated hardy for specific gardening zones are able to survive year in and year out without intervention from humans. Beginning with earliest life, plants have survived by genetically adjusting to ever-changing environments. Adapt or die has always been, and still is, the creed of life. As a result, the hardy plants of today's world have survived by acclimating themselves to withstand the bitter cold of northern climates, or the life-threatening heat and droughts in warm regions of the temperate zones (areas of the world that are warm in the summer, cold in the winter and mild in spring and fall).

However, temperature and precipitation amounts are not the only criteria for hardiness. Plant hardiness is also influenced by a number of other factors such as humidity, seasonal winds, soils and location within localized ecosystems. Half-hardy plants may make it through a bitter cold winter, only to succumb in the spring from a late freeze-thaw cycle. It can be quite tricky to figure out the microclimates within your personal ecosystems. However, after a few years of experimentation, you can usually figure out what works best in your small gardening world.

DORMANCY

This book is concerned exclusively with garden areas which experience seasonal change accompanied by some form of cold-induced dormancy. During this dormant period, metabolic activity is greatly reduced and can take a number of forms, from deciduous plants dropping leaves, to evergreens simply slowing their metabolism, to bulbs retreating underground.

Plants which thrive in these regions take their cues from day length and temperature. Their instinct for dormancy is so fixed that they rarely survive if moved to a climatic zone that varies too greatly from their present one. For example, most bulbs require a period of cold weather before they initiate new growth in the springtime. They awaken only after a period of dormancy and are simply incapable of reprogramming themselves. They either die or become half-hardy or tender when exposed to temperatures to which they are unaccustomed.

In order to survive cold dormant periods, hardy plants have developed the ability to withstand fatal damage at the cellular level. As temperatures drop, plant cells move water out of their centers and into the outer sections of each cell. This process leaves a highly concentrated sap in the center of the cell, the part that matters the most. This sap has a lower freezing point than pure water and therefore does not freeze as fast as the outer, more watery cell layers. Half-hardy and tender plants lack this ability to migrate water outwards. Entire cells freeze, causing them to burst and die. If too many cells are affected, the entire plant succumbs.

PLANT HARDINESS ZONE MAPS

The most commonly used plant hardiness zone map in the United States is compiled by the United Stated Department of Agriculture (USDA). This map divides the United States into 10 zones of plant hardiness and is the hardiness map most commonly accepted by the American horticulture industry. The map presented for Europe was compiled using the same criteria as for the United States map. However, Western Europe is broken into less zones because it suffers fewer weather extremes.

Zone maps base their divisions on the consistent, annual, minimum temperatures plants must endure each year in order to survive. These maps always make the assumption that moisture amounts and nutrient levels remain adequate.

However, zone maps present only the broadest picture. They neglect to take into account many other factors such as precipitation, wind, humidity levels, and snowfall, all of which impact plant hardiness. In the United States, winter conditions are strongly influenced by the vast land and ice mass to its north. As cold air radiates south from the Arctic, it is tempered in various ways by mountain ranges, the oceans to the east and west, the Great Lakes and even the waters of the Gulf

of Mexico. And to further complicate things, the western half of the United States experiences its own weather patterns caused by the unstable air constantly flowing off the Pacific Ocean, and by the fact that the West contains a disproportionate amount of deserts and mountain ranges. To gain a better understanding of the many microclimates that exist in the western half of the United States, consult the hardiness map put out by Sunset Magazine. This magazine divides the western states into no less than 24 climate zones.

Zone Map: Visit the following web site for plant hardiness zone maps and further information on climate zones. The site includes the USDA Zone Map as well as the zone map created by *Sunset Magazine*. This site will give you a greater understanding of zone maps and why they are such an invaluable resource for all gardeners.

http://doityourself.com/gardenmaint/agardenersguidetozonemaps.htm

The climate in Europe is influenced in a similar manner as North America. The cold Asian air mass to the east of Europe is offset by the combined warming influences of the Atlantic Ocean and the Sahara Desert. Western Europe enjoys a much milder climate than Eastern Europe because it is closer to the Atlantic, and as a result, benefits greatly from the warming affects of the Gulf Stream. Due to this phenomenon, the semi-tropical gardens in southwest England resemble the lush gardens of the Mediterranean, and gardens as far north as Scandinavia rarely experience killing frosts.

HOW LOCALIZED CONDITIONS AFFECT PLANT HARDINESS

A wide range of factors, such as altitude, flatness or slope of ground, soil type, nearness of a large body of water, and buildings all affect local climates. Among these, altitude has the most influence on determining minimum temperatures within individual zones. *A rough guide to follow is that for every 250 feet (100 meters) a garden rises up a hill, the temperature drops by one degree Fahrenheit.*

Also, gardens located on hilltops, or on north or west facing slopes, are more prone to damage from high winds. The stronger the wind, the more a plant is vulnerable to desiccation (dry out). At extremely high altitudes, little plant life exists except for those plant species which have adapted to a constant barrage of punishing winds.

Conversely, while gardens located in valleys are well out of the path of winds, they are more subject to killing frosts. Cold air slides downward on frosty nights and deposits pockets of freezing air into low-lying valleys. Plants growing in bottomland must be able to withstand freeze-thaw cycles on a regular basis. Therefore, valleys are poor sites for half-hardy plants whose tender, springtime buds and shoots are sitting ducks for killing frosts.

Try to avoid planting half-hardy plants on the south side of a hill. Southern slopes are tempered by the sun which causes plants to come to life faster than those grown on northern slopes. This puts half-hardy plants in jeopardy because of the widely fluctuating temperatures of late fall and early spring. It is important to pick plants for south facing hillsides that are tough enough to withstand the extremes of hot sunlight and frosty nights.

A house and its surrounding landmass create their own climatic pockets. The combination of sunshine and wind on the south and west sides of buildings dries out plants much faster than on other sides. Also, when wind hits buildings at right angles, it drops half of its force downward, which can wreak havoc on vulnerable plants.

On the other hand, walls warmed by the sun act as heat reservoirs and can be great places to grow deciduous plants. At Muddy Creek, the crocuses located in beds along the south side of our house come into flower in February, or as soon as the snow melts. On the north side, where the snow-covered beds are blanketed in shadow until late in the day, the crocuses bloom much later. In other words, our front beds are probably a half or full zone warmer than the beds on the north side of the house.

It is important to be careful when choosing plants for the sunny side of your house because its southern exposure can put half-hardy plants at risk of dying from rapid thawing. Half-hardy plants are simply not capable of percolating water back into their outer cells quickly enough to prevent fatal cell damage during fast melt downs.

Cities create their own microclimates because they contain copious amounts of structural mass. The warmth stored in buildings, streets, sidewalks and other heat retaining components keeps air and soil temperatures higher than in the surrounding countryside.

The type of soil in your garden beds also influences plant hardiness. Heavy soils are much slower to heat up or cool down. Conversely, light, sandy soils trap more air, which in turns acts as an insulator between the atmosphere and the heat stored in the ground. *As a result, soils kept light by regular applications of decomposed organic matter do a much better job of protecting roots during the winter months.*

HOW PLANTS PREPARE
FOR THE DORMANT SEASON

All temperate zone plants encounter periods of freezing weather from time to time and can suffer some form of damage if unprepared. Freezing in nature is a normal and gradual process, but plants need time to get ready for it. The warm days and cool nights in autumn create a toughening-up period. Plants program themselves to slow down their nighttime transpiration and to store extra carbohydrates in their tissues as protection against freezing. This metabolic slowdown allows them to spend more energy preparing for winter instead of continuing to put forth new growth.

Deciduous shrubs and trees shed their soft, vulnerable leaves because leaves become a detriment in the wintertime. Leaves need to remain hydrated and they would demand water at a time when frozen roots are incapable of responding. Deciduous plants also harden any wood which hasn't reached a safe state of ripeness (more brown than green) to prevent cellular damage during frigid weather. This is why pruning should never be done too close to winter as it can stimulate woody plants to put on new growth at the wrong time of the year.

Evergreen plants hold on to their leaves, but they lessen their transpiration rate (rate water is lost through leaf evaporation) by partially shuting the pores in their leaves. This metabolic slowdown is vital to their survival because frozen roots are unable to replace moisture lost through leaf evaporation. Evergreens would suffer severe desiccation if they had not developed this winter survival tactic. As further protection, many evergreen species have thick (often shiny and/or waxy) leaves which have been genetically engineered to protect them from water loss.

Bulbs and other tubular-rooted plants withdraw all their food supplies to their plump larders well below the soil's surface. Unless they are discovered and pried out by four-legged scavengers, they slumber peacefully until the warmth of spring awakens them.

PREPARING GARDENS
FOR THE DORMANT SEASON

All plants, trees and shrubs, especially newly planted ones, should be given adequate water throughout the fall to ensure they enter the dormant season well hydrated. Pay particular attention to evergreens because they still lose some water though their leaves, and therefore have a higher desiccation rate than deciduous plants.

As soon as the soil in your garden beds becomes deeply frozen, cover vulnerable plants with a two- to six-inch layer of protective mulch such as compost, pine needles, whole evergreen boughs, straw (not hay; it drops a lot of seed), well-shredded leaves or whatever suitable material you have on hand. Take special care to avoid smothering the crowns of small perennials which can promote fungal diseases. Mulch helps soils maintain even temperatures and cuts down on water loss throughout the winter months. Heavy frosts followed by thaws tend to heave plants out of the ground. Shallow-rooted or newly planted perennials are especially at risk. Protective coverings keep damage from frost heaves or rapid thaws to a minimum. Be sure to keep this winter cover on until all danger of spring frosts has passed.

In colder regions, broadleaf evergreens, such as boxwood, rhododendrons and azaleas are particularly prone to desiccation from strong winds and periods of intense winter sunlight. Vulnerable plants can be protected by wrapping them in burlap or by erecting wind breaks. Terry and I drape our small boxwood parterre

with burlap, weighing down the ends with bricks or rocks. As a result, we rarely experience winterkill because the burlap deters the boxwood from drying out. Synthetic landscape fleeces offer a nice alternative to burlap. They are lighter in weight than burlap and allow plenty of light, air and water to pass through. Also, unlike burlap, they do not rot, shrink or break down under ultraviolet rays. If stored properly, landscape fleece should last quite a few seasons.

Man-made windbreaks are an excellent means of protecting plants which lie in the path of high winds. These breaks act just like trees and can greatly reduce the velocity of the wind. Try to place them at least 6 to 8 feet back from the plants. The idea is to block the wind but still allow room for air to circulate. These fences are usually made of synthetic fabric attached to fence posts. By multiplying the length times the width of the fence, you can determine how much area will be protected. A fence with an area of 75 square feet will provide wind protection of 6 to 10 times that area.

Another way to protect broadleaf evergreens is to apply anti-desiccant sprays. These sprays are made of organic, biodegradable materials which form a protective coating over an entire plant and are capable of reducing moisture loss by up to 80 percent. They act as sealants to keep moisture in but are porous enough to allow leaves to breath. They should be applied in late fall on a day when temperatures are warmer than 40°F. A second application may be applied on a mild February day if temperatures rise above 40°F.

When removing heavy accumulations of snow from the branches of unprotected shrubs and trees, carefully push snow upward and gently shake individual branches. Large evergreen shrubs can be wrapped in spirals of twine just like Christmas trees prepared for transport. This allows snow to slide downward instead of lodging in branches where it can cause irreparable damage.

In areas that experience heavy snowfall, other types of perennial shrubs also benefit from extra precautions.. Daphnes, for instance, open at their tops as they age which exposes their fragile branches to breakage from heavy snow accumulations. There are four daphne shrubs in my front border garden, and each one of them is dear to me. Having lost entire sections of the older ones, I try to find the time to place small wooden A-frames over them in winter. These wooden tents are very easy to make by buying inexpensive plywood and cutting pieces to the correct size for each shrub. The pieces are then hinged together at the top, creating a two-sided tent so that air and moisture can still circulate through the open ends. They fold flat and can be easily stored when not in use.

Our dogs keep most of the voles, moles, rabbits and deer on the run. However, in my new woodland garden, I will soon find out if I'll need to take extra precautions against wildlife. These creatures love to chew on bark, especially in winter when most of their regular food supplies are buried in deep snow. The cambium layer, which lies just under the bark of woody plants, contains the vessels which pass water and nutrients back and forth between the roots and the above ground parts.

If the bark on trunks is chewed all the way around (girdled), irreparably damaging the cambium layer, the entire shrub or tree

will die. Plants that have been partially girdled are prone to invasion by disease or borers (various types of beetle and caterpillar larvae) seeking freshly exposed plant tissue. Many garden centers sell a variety of plastic collars and tapes to wrap around woody trunks to deter four-legged pests. Sprays and paints are also available, but I personally prefer to use natural, nontoxic methods of control.

Ancient celebrations shed light on the
darkness of the winter solstice.

DECEMBER

Ornaments, Favorite Books,
Nurseries, and Suppliers

s December arrives with its winter stillness, I gratefully pause to reflect upon the past gardening year. As I wander the gardens cutting boughs of evergreens and searching for interesting seed heads, a feeling of peaceful satisfaction settles over me. While I cut and clip, I feel so grateful that I live in Vermont, where the harshness of winter forces me to take time off. I marvel at gardeners in tropical climates who must care for their gardens 12 months of the year. Ardent passions need periods of respite; otherwise they may be consumed by the very fire that fuels them.

So, I happily turn my thoughts to the holidays with all of its festivities and celebrations. I throw my energies into wreath- and cookie-making, gift-wrapping and the myriad of other chores that come with the season. I blatantly drop gift hints to Terry, such as giving him lists of books and garden magazines I can no longer live without or new tools to replace those recycled with the compost or lost under a shrub.

In this chapter, I would like to share some resources, from books to garden-supply companies to nurseries. The books, nurseries, and garden-supply companies that have made this list are my favorites. They are the ones which have given me the greatest inspiration or quality of product.

Happy holidays!

DECORATING WITH NATURAL MATERIALS

Many years ago my daughters and I lived in Pennsylvania within a few miles of Chadds Ford. Each year, one of the highlights of the holiday season was visiting the Brandywine River Museum which showcases three generations of paintings by the Wyeth family. The museum, housed in an old stone mill on the banks of the Brandywine River, is the perfect venue for the art produced by this extraordinary family.

During the holiday season, however, our main reason for visiting the museum was not to look at the paintings, but rather to step back into time. Each year, an entire room on the first floor was transformed into a scene right out of a Victorian novel, with miniature people arrayed in old-fashioned finery, children skating and sledding, and elaborate trains winding through snowy fields and small towns. As whistles tooted and vendors hawked their wares, we never ceased to be filled with rapture.

My favorite feature of all was the immense tree standing on the old cobblestone floor in the entry hall. My breath was taken away the first time I saw it. It was covered from top to bottom with ornaments made entirely from nature's remnants. Seed pods, deadheads, pine cones, corn husks and all kinds of dried plant material had been fashioned into animals of all descriptions. I soon found myself with pen in hand sketching as many ornaments as I could so the girls and I could make our own. While ours were not quite as cleverly made, they graced our tree for many years thereafter. Each year, when I find little pieces of these creatures at the bottom of our Christmas boxes, I am taken back to those magical years.

Below are some sketches by Hannah of these ornaments. I hope they will start your artistic juices flowing, just as they did mine many years ago.

FAVORITE GARDEN BOOKS

The books highlighted here are those that have given me the most insight into the practice of caring for perennial plants. But more than that, they have led me into the inner sanctum of fellow plant lovers. Even though I garden in isolation, it is the inspiration I receive from my readings that guides my gardening life here at Muddy Creek.

Caring for Perennials: What to Do and When to Do It by Janet Macunovich
(Storey Publishing, 1997)

Janet is a designer, teacher, garden writer and an expert in every aspect of caring for ornamental perennials. This book is based upon Janet's experience tending an individual garden bed at a university botanical garden for a full gardening year. What I particularly loved about this book is how each plant becomes her friend as she tends its every need over the course of the growing season. As Janet cares for these plants, almost every aspect of caring for perennials comes into play. This was one of the first books I read after acquiring my gardens, and it was instrumental in providing a solid foundation for my subsequent years of gardening at Muddy Creek.

The Well-Tended Perennial Garden by Tracy DiSabato-Aus
(Timber Press, 1998)

Tracy is a horticultural consultant, designer, writer and lecturer. This book is one of the best guides to planting and pruning that I have read. What makes this book an especially useful tool for gardeners is its extensive encyclopedia of the important perennial species and cultivars. This section takes up more than half the book and includes specific pruning and maintenance information on

each plant. Tracy also includes extensive appendices which list plants according to a wide range of horticultural needs, such as soil type, division requirements, resistance to disease and a number of other factors. This book was invaluable to me during my early gardening years and will continue to be a main resource for years to come.

The Principles of Gardening by Hugh Johnson (Simon & Schuster, 1997)

Hugh is a world-renowned gardener. He was a founder of *The Plantsman,* a British horticultural magazine, and for years wrote a monthly column for the *New York Times* called "The Gardener's Eye." There is no better read on the market if your goal is to acquire a close understanding of the gardening world. It is the perfect book for gardeners who thirst for more knowledge and yet do not wish to become botanists.

The following quote is just one of many wonderful insights and opinions Hugh shares with his readers: "A poet is limited to the dictionary, a sculptor starts with a block of stone, but a gardener starts with a plot that is frozen one day and flooded the next, here in sun and there in shadow, teased by wind and tantalized by drought, plagued by insects, toyed with by birds, mined by moles. Many gardeners are intimidated by painting or writing and yet in choosing to create a garden, they take on one of the most complex art forms of all."

Beth Chatto's Woodland Garden: Shade-Loving Plants for Year-Round Interest by Beth Chatto and Illustrated by Steven Wooster (Cassell Illustrated, 2002)

Written in Beth Chatto's engaging personal style, this book offered a wealth of practical information to me when I designed my woodland garden at Muddy Creek. Having visited Beth's famous gardens in East Anglia, England, I saw first hand the woodland garden that she and her husband created years ago from their scrubby, hurricane-ravished woods. They transformed this woodland into a garden filled with life and vigor, drawing on Beth's artistic eye for color, form and shape, and her forty-plus years of demonstrating how problem areas can be seen as opportunities. This book was inspirational to me and turned the trials and tribulations of planting in shade into a wondrous experience. I'm sure that every gardener who loves shade gardening will be inspired by the magical plant combinations and palette of woodland-loving perennials shared so beautifully in this book.

Dear Friend and Gardener: Letters on Life and Gardening by Beth Chatto and
Christopher Lloyd (Frances Lincoln, 1998)

"This is a wonderful book, a celebration of friendship, optimism, hard work,
gaiety, doggedness, and the possibilities of sudden and unexpected revelation."
Even though these words were written by *Country Life* magazine and not by me, I
couldn't agree with them more. As a young man, Lloyd inherited a famous garden
at Great Dixter in Sussex, England. After taking a degree in horticulture at Wye
College, he came home and threw his boundless energies into making the Great
Dixter gardens distinctively his own. Lloyd became famous for his plantsmanship,
and he has a daring imagination which he is never afraid to use. This is especially
evident in his famous borders where reds, oranges and purples planted in his
free-wheeling style test the eye's limits for contrast and discord.

Beth Catto is also one of the world's most valued and influential gardeners.
Her gardens and nursery in East Anglia are particularly inspiring because she
and her husband literally transformed a bog-ridden low land and its surrounding
sun-baked gravel soils into one of the finest gardens of modern day. This was
accomplished by choosing and growing plants that were adapted by nature for
the difficult soil conditions they were asked to grow in. Beth Chatto's garden is a
testament to the ingenuity and perseverance of two remarkable gardeners against
all odds. It is a brilliant example of ecological sensitivity and should encourage
all of us to *grow the right plant in the right spot.*

This endearing book kept me company for several months as I rationed out
a few letters to read per night. In doing so, I felt as if I had briefly entered the
lives of these two influential and remarkable gardeners.

The Botany of Desire: A Plant's-Eye View of the World by Michael Pollan
(Random House, 2001)

In this thought-provoking and eye-opening book, Michael Pollan links four
fundamental human desires — sweetness, beauty, intoxication, and control — with
plants that satisfy them: the apple, the tulip, marijuana, and the potato. He uses
these familiar species to make the case that the evolution of these plants may have
been influenced by man's need to satiate these desires. He leads you to believe
that some plants may possess the "genetic smarts" to manipulate human beings
into perpetuating their existence. I particularly loved this book because of Pollan's
subversive streak and his ability to root out counterintuitive ideas. However, I
must give readers a word of warning. After reading Pollan's section on the potato,
I never again want to eat any potato that is not organically grown!

Ghosts in the Garden: Reflections on Endings, Beginnings, and the Unearthing of Self by Beth Kephart with photographs by William Sulit (New World Library, 2005)

Beth Kephart's memoir on personal growth was a National Book Award nominee in 2005. Ghosts in the Garden is an insightful meditation on aging, identity, and memory set against the back-drop of the Chanticleer garden in south-eastern Pennsylvania. Dedicated to "those who love the smell of the earth and the color of a bloom upon a tree," Beth's book shares her two-year self-exploration in one of the world's most celebrated pleasure gardens. She was a stranger to the gardening world at the beginning of her weekly visits to the garden, but intuitively she knew that she had found her way to a place that could teach her about life. She strikes up friendships with gardeners and visitors, she sits waiting for owls on night-time visits, but most of all she is drawn to the deep calm she feels whenever she is in the garden. William Sulit's sensitive black-and-white photographs are the perfect accompaniment for this beautifully written book.

FAVORITE TOOL SOURCES
AND GARDEN SUPPLY COMPANIES

Gardener's Supply Company, The Intervale, Burlington, Vermont 05401
Phone: 888-833-1412 Web: www.gardeners.com

This premier garden company was founded by Will Raap, the leading visionary behind the reclamation of a farming area known as the Intervale, which lies within the city limits of Burlington. This rich bottomland with 700 years of farming history had become a dumping ground for the city. Will Rapp had the vision to involve the community in cleaning up and revitalizing this unique natural re-

source. Thanks to his initial efforts, this entire area is now under the stewardship of the nonprofit Intervale Foundation which helps fund and oversee a number of farming projects presently operating on this reclaimed land. Visitors who walk or bike through the area can visit more than a dozen market gardens, a community garden, a native plant nursery and a compost facility which produces more than 10,000 tons of finished compost each year. This Intervale bike trail links up with the 10-mile Cycle-the-City loop.

When Will opened Gardener's Supply in 1983, he located it in the Intervale where he knew there would be ample room to fulfill his vision of creating a first-rate nursery and garden supply company. Since its conception, this company has grown into one of the top garden supply companies in the United States. Their extensive catalog showcases every type of gardening tool imaginable, as well as countless other valuable items and accessories from all over the world. The Burlington retail store features a year-round greenhouse full of orchids and other exotics and culinary herbs. The nursery offers a wide selection of perennials, roses, ground covers, shrubs, and trees throughout the growing season.

Gardener's Supply is also the U.S. home for Dutch Gardens, a mail order company that has been importing Dutch flower bulbs for more than 50 years. You can see these bulbs in flower as you wander through the acre display garden which also features wildflowers, water gardens, edible plants, perennials and annuals. If you live within driving distance of Burlington, think about spending a few days of vacation time in this small city on Lake Champlain. It is a vibrant place with lots of culture and outdoor activities. All summer long there is a booming farmer's market on Saturdays, as well as street performers, good food of all types, and great craft shopping. Then you can drive to Gardeners Supply and load up your car before heading home. It's my idea of a perfect vacation.

Gardens Alive, 5100 Schenley Place, Lawrenceburg, IN 47025
Phone: 513-354-1483 Web: www.gardensalive.com

For two decades, this company has searched for, tested, and introduced environmentally responsible gardening products that really work. Their catalog is filled with organic-based products for conscientious gardeners who wish to protect themselves and their environment from chemical pollutants.

I have learned so much by reading their catalog. It gives extensive descriptions explaining how and why each product works. You learn all about most of the common garden pests because the catalog contains an 18-page illustrated guide with photos, descriptions and organic solutions for most of the main garden bugs and

diseases. Their products include a wide range of items such as bagged compost, soil test kits, beneficial nematodes for the soil, compost aerators, lady-bird beetles, Escar-Go!® slug and snail control, garlic clips to repel deer and rabbits, compost tea kits, red worms, and defense patches to stick on your hat during deer fly season. This is the perfect source for dealing organically with any garden problem that might arise. A special bonus of 10 percent off any purchases is offered to customers who join their Stay Organic Garden Club for $9.95 per year.

Lee Valley Tools, Ltd., P.O. Box 1780, Ogdensburg, NY 13669-6780
Phone: 800-871-8158 Web: www.leevalley.com

This company offers a wide range of hard-to-find tools and gadgets of all types and descriptions. You'll find such things as refractometers (which test when fruits and vegetables are ripe for harvesting), Japanese folding Dozuki saws, sundials, bird feeders, Felco® pruners, automatic plant waterers and a myriad of other unusual items.

Lee Valley also specializes in unique gifts for inquisitive-minded friends and loved ones. Their catalogs are such fun to read. Many happy hours can be spent picking out unusual items for almost any gift-giving occasion.

Smith & Hawken, Ltd., P.O. Box 8690, Pueblo, CO 81008
Phone: 800-940-1170 Web: www.smith-hawken.com

Smith & Hawken is known for its elegant patio furniture, garden benches, trellises and fencing. Their catalogs are a feast for the eyes, and over the years I have spent many hours daydreaming over their wonderful selection of decorative garden items. They also offer a choice selection of plants, as well as tools, garden pots, fountains, birdbaths, and decorative hose holders to mention just a few. For my 50th birthday, my four daughters gave me a teak garden bench with a brass engraved plate commemorating the occasion. It was a time when none of us had much money and yet they chose to go to Smith & Hawken for my gift. After years of watching me spend hours engrossed in their catalogs, they knew how much I would appreciate having one of their benches.

FAVORITE NURSERIES

Horsford Garden and Nursery, Route 7, Charlotte, Vermont 05445
Phone:802-425-2811 Web:www.horsfordnursery.com
Owners: Charlie Prout and Eileen Schilling

Horsfords is the nursery that year-in and year-out has become the mainstay for the bulk of my plant purchases. Founded in the late 1920's by F.H. Horsford, this first-rate plant nursery was bought by Eileen and Charlie in 1986. In 2005, Horsfords reintroduced the "Regal Plant" concept which was first introduced by the original owner as a "brand of plants associated with health and superior growth." To

quote F.H. Horsford from his 1935 catalog, "Regal plants grow a little taller, bloom a little longer, flower a little more profusely. If you find they serve you better (and we believe you will) much of the credit must be given to the hardiness that the soil and sunshine of our little Vermont valley has put into them."

Eileen and Charlie's efforts over the last eighteen years refining growing techniques, perfecting plant selection, and evaluating plants throughout Vermont has surely earned them the right to reinstate the "Regal Plant" concept at Horsfords. They have one of the friendliest and most helpful staffs of any nursery I visit and always go the extra mile when I ask them for assistance. Kudos to all of you at Horsfords for providing our corner of Vermont with a top-drawer nursery in all respects.

Rocky Dale Gardens, 806 Rocky Dale Road, Bristol, VT 05443
Phone: 802-453-2782 Web: www.rockydalegardens.com

In 2002, this outstanding nursery and gardens was turned over to its new owner, Ed Burke. Having been inspired by the previous owners, Holly Weir and Bill Pollard, for many years prior to acquiring Rocky Dale, Ed is continuing in their tradition of offering first-rate plants that have been proven hardy for our northern climate. Rocky Dale also specializes in unusual and hard-to-find plants, including exotic annuals. I go to Rocky Dale if I am looking for a rare woodland plant, unusual conifer or a Japanese maple tough enough to weather our winters.

I acquired one of my favorite plants there last year, *Petasites japonicus* 'Giganteus', which I had first seen in the North Hill garden of Joe Eck and Wayne Winterrowd in southern Vermont. This wetland-loving plant emerges in early spring with curious, chartreuse flowers which are a feast for the eyes. It then goes on to grow immense leaves which have led to its pet name of "poor man's gunnera." For me it is like bringing a bit of England to my gardens at Muddy Creek. *However, this plant is highly invasive, so it must be planted where it can't overrun its boundaries. I have since moved it to a spot where I'm sure it will stay put. In other words, between a rock and a hard place!*

One of the highlights of visiting this nursery is the display garden which backs up to a rocky cliff covered with mosses, lichens and ferns. The stunning beauty of the natural setting and the manner in which the garden is laid out at the foot of these massive rocks makes this garden a delight to visit. Located just 20 minutes north of Middlebury, Vermont, on the edge of the charming village of Bristol, Rocky Dale should be added to your list of first-rate nurseries to visit in New England.

Cady's Falls Nursery, 637 Duhamel Road, Morrisville, VT 05661
Phone: 802-888-5559 e-mail:averycfn@sover.net
Owners: Don and Lela Avery

Don and Lela have been in the nursery business for 25 years. Over the last two decades, Cady's Falls has played an important role in the horticultural awakening that has occurred in Vermont. To quote Don and Lela, "We feel fortunate to have played a part in overcoming the geographical and mental isolation that separates us from the rich horticultural tradition of the more temperate world." Gardening in New England, with its severe winters, makes it necessary to grow plants that are garden hardy; thus Cady's Falls plants not only look good, but they can be trusted to withstand the harsh climatic conditions of northern New England. Don and Lela summerize it well when they say, "We need perennials whose roots and crowns won't rot in months of cold mud and we need woody plants that won't tear apart under the weight of snow and mud. And perhaps more important, we need plants that harden up in the early fall and are not tricked out of dormancy by a January thaw."

My daughter Heather introduced me to this special nursery years ago, and I was instantly enamored by it. Besides offering a large and eclectic assortment of plants displayed next to an ancient barn, Don and Lela actually live on the property and have surrounded themselves with world-class gardens of their own making. My favorite section is the stream garden which features a vast array of plant material, ranging from rock garden plants to shade plants to water-loving plants. I always arrive early so I can wander through the gardens and still not miss out on buying before someone takes just the plant I was looking for. If you are looking for dwarf and unusual conifers, this is a great place to visit. Because they are always seeking something new and different, Don and Lela continually propagate new conifers, and in many cases these conifers are new to American horticulture. In fact, over 90% of all the plants sold at Cady's Falls are propagated at their nursery. So even if you must drive quite a distance to get there, it is well worth the trip. The charming village of Stowe is just 20 minutes south of Cady's Falls and is a wonderful place to spend the night and explore art galleries, shops, indulge in good food and soak up the ambience of the Green Mountains.

Heronswood Nursery, Ltd., 7530 NE 288th Street, Kingston, WA 98346
Phone: 360-297-4172 Web: www.heronswood .com
Owners: W. Atlee Burpee

All gardeners should know about this nursery. Not only do they sell hard-to-find plant species, but interspersed throughout their extensive plant catalog are short essays written by some of the top garden writers of today. To quote Helen Dillon's words in the 2000 catalog regarding her love of the Heronswood catalog: "What is it about a Heronswood catalog that I find so endearing? Apart from the beauty of the Jean Emmon's watercolor cover, start to flick through — and if you are not immediately hooked by the list of plants, you certainly will be by Dan's stupendous list of adjectives, unequalled in North America. If a suitable one doesn't exist, he simply makes one up — Indigoferaceous indeed. Here in Ireland I find a Heronswood catalog particularly useful to wave at American visitors as I'm laying down the law. It gives me intense pleasure to point out that not only is the Trillium/uvularia/smilacina a native of North America where they come from, but curiously enough the plant is easily available. Just apply to Heronswood. This immediately puts a stop to people bleating about a plant being unavailable. At this point you can tell which visitors are serious — these are the ones that immediately get out a notebook for the address. Others look rather shifty and pretend huge interest in a passing bumblebee — making an effort to write for a plant is not their thing."

Heronswood holds a number of seminars each year which they list in their catalog. All nursery visitors who purchase plants are given the special priviledge of touring their private gardens. The gardens are open to the public six days of the year and one of my lifetime wishes is to visit Heronswood. Poor Terry. So many of our trips around the world are driven by proximity to great gardens.

Garden in the Woods, 180 Hemenway Road, Framingham, MA 01701
Phone: 508-877-7630 Web: www.newfs.org

Garden in the Woods is the horticultural gem of the New England Wild Flower Society and one of America's great botanical gardens. This woodland garden is a sanctuary for more than 1,500 species and cultivars, some of which are so rare you may be seeing them for the first time. The garden is designed to educate and inspire visitors about native plants and their conservation. "Native" means any plant species that was growing in North America before the European colonists arrived.

The garden has a one-mile loop trail that takes you through a diverse ecological landscape. It consists of a rich woodland full of wildflowers, ferns and native rhododendrons, a lily pond with wetland-loving plants, turtles, frogs and insects; a western garden displaying plants native to regions west of the Mississippi River; and a wildflower meadow chock-full of native grasses, wildflowers, birds, butterflies and insects. There is also a series of small gardens featuring native plants which have adapted to unusual conditions. This series of miniature ecosystems includes a bog, a Tufa rock (limestone) garden, a pine barrens, an acid slope and a fascinating pitcher plant display. When Terry and I visited Garden in the Woods recently, it was such a delight to see parents introducing their young children to the many wonders of this natural garden. And I found that I was as childlike as the children when I envisioned myself as a struggling bug trapped inside the dark, slimy interior of a pitcher plant.

The nursery is known for its wide selection of unusual and rare native plants, and is open from mid-April through September. The sales area is literally bursting with a multitude of plants to fill any northern gardener's dreams. They also have a lovely gift shop filled with garden books and gifts. It is especially comforting to buy from this nursery because all purchases support the regional plant conservation mission of the New England Wildflower Society. Since Garden in the Woods does not ship plants, this is another chance to base a vacation around a fun city and a visit to an outstanding garden and nursery. As Terry and I drove out of Boston on our most recent visit, it's a wonder the police didn't pull us over. It looked as if our car had been commandeered by an army of plants bent on escaping to the country.

Completely Clematis Specialty Nursery, 217 Argilla Road, Ipswich, MA 01938
Phone: 978-356-3197 Web: www.clematisnursury.com
Owner: Susan Austin

This specialty nursery has supplied me with a number of wonderful clematis plants over the past few years. Since it is almost impossible to cultivate climbing roses here in northern Vermont, many of us plant clematis in their stead. And even though our climate is too harsh for clematis to ramble over entire houses as they do in England, they add an enchanting aura to gardens as they climb trellises, thread their way up lilacs, or any other support system you choose to

provide. Completely Clematis has endless plants to select from, and I love perusing their catalog for new plants. But my favorite thing about this company is their knowledge and passion for clematis which they are more than eager to share with prospective buyers. The owner, Sue Austin, was very friendly and helpful to me when I put in my first big order. Not only did she give me lots of specific growing tips but recommended some terrific books, my favorite of which is *Clematis: The Genus* by Christopher Grey-Wilson (Timber Press, 2000). They sell a few of the best clematis books on the market and also offer clematis-adorned pots, dishes and note cards. This is definitely the place to shop if you are searching for hard-to-find clematis plants raised with expert and loving care.

References

Alden, Peter, and Brian Cassie. *National Audubon Society — Field Guide to New England*. New York: Alfred A. Knopf, 1998.

American Horticultural Society. *Encyclopedia of Garden Plants*. London: Dorling Kindersley Limited, 1989.

Ball, Jeff and Liz Ball. *Rodale's Landscape Problem Solver*. Emmaus, Pennsylvania: Rodale Press, 1989.

Brooks, Audrey, and Andrew Halstead. *Garden Pests and Diseases*. London, England: Octopus Publishing Group,1999.

Brookes, John. *The Book of Garden Design*. London, England: Dorling Kindersley, 1991.

Brookes, John. *Garden Masterclass*. London, England: Dorling Kindersley, 2002.

Cabot, Francis H. *The Greater Perfection*. New York: W.W. Norton, 2001.

Capon, Brian. *Botany for Gardeners*. Portland, Oregon: Timber Press, 1990.

Carr, Anna, and Linda Gilkeson, Miranda Smith. *Insect, Disease and Weed I.D. Guide*. Emmaus, Pennsylvania: Rodale Press, 2001.

Cole, Trevor. *American Horticultural Society — Northeast-Smart Garden Regional Guide*. New York: DK Publishing, 2003.

Craigmyle, Marshall. *Perennials — The Comprehensive Guide to over 2700 Plants*. Leeds, England: Colin Gower Enterprises, 2003.

Cullina, William. *The New England Wild Flower Society Guide to Growing and Propagating Wildflowers of the United States and Canada*. Boston-New York: Houghton Mifflin Company, 2000.

Darke, Rick. *The American Woodland Garden*. Portland, Oregon: Timber Press, 2002.

DiSabato-Aust, Tracy. *The Well-Tended Perennial Garden*. Portland, Oregon:Timber Press, 1998.

Druse, Ken. *The Natural Garden*. New York: Clarkson N. Potter, 1989.

Eck, Joe, and Wayne Winterrowd. *A Year at North Hill*. Boston: Little, Brown and Co., 1995.

Eyewitness Handbooks. *Garden Trees*. New York: DK Publishing, 1996.

Fell, Derek. *The Essential Gardner*. New York: Crescent Books, 1990.

Gates, Galen, and Chris Graham, Ethan Johnson. *Shrubs and Vines*. New York: Pantheon Books, 1994.

Gershuny, Grace, and Deborah L.Martin (Editors). *The Rodale Book of Composting*. Emmaus, Pennsylvania: Rodale Press, 1992.

Grey-Wilson. *Clematis the Genus*. Portland, Oregon: Timber Press, 2000.

Hattatt, Lance. *Encyclopedia of Garden Plants and Flowers*. Bath, England: Paragon Publishing, 1998.

Hobhouse, Penelope. *A Book of Gardening*. Boston, Massachusetts: Little, Brown and Company, 1986.

Ingram, David S., and Peter J. Gregory, Daphne Vince-Prue (Editors). *Science and the Garden*. Oxford, England: Blackwell Science Ltd., 2002.

Johnson, Hugh. *The Principles of Gardening*. New York: Simon & Schuster, 1979.

Kourik, Robert. *Pruning*. New York: Workman Publishing, 1997.

MacCaskey, Mike with Bill Marken and the Editors of the National Gardening Association. *Gardening for Dummies*. Foster City, California: IDG Books Worldwide, 1999.

Macunovich, Janet. *Caring for Perennials; What to do and When to do it*. North Adams, Massachusetts: Storey Books, 1996.

Martin, Tovah. *Tasha Tudor's Garden*. New York: Houghton Mifflin Company, 1994.

McDonals, Elvin. *The 100 Best Trees and Shrubs*. New York: Random House, 1995.

Mikolajski, Andrew. *How to Get Rid of Garden Pests and Diseases*. London, England: Hermes House, 2004.

Phillips, Rodger, and Martyn Rix. *Perennials (Volumes 1 & 2)*. London, England: Macmillan, 1996.

Reich, Lee. *The Pruning Book*. Newtown, Connecticut: Taunton Press, 1999.

Roth, Sally. *Natural Landscaping- Gardening with Nature to Create a Backyard Paradise*. Emmaus, Pennsylvania: Rodale Press, 1997.

Shenk, George. *Moss Gardening*. Portland, Oregon: Timber Press, 1997.

Shenk, George. *The Complete Shade Gardener*. Portland, Oregon: Timber Press, 1984.

Squire, David. *Pruning Basics*. New York: Sterling Publishing Company, Inc., 2001.

Tanner, Ogden. *Living Fences*. Shelburne, Vermont: Chapters Publishing Ltd., 1995.

Toomey, Mary, and Everett Leeds. *An Illustrated Encyclopedia of Clematis*. Portland, Oregon: Timber Press, 2001.

Index

aMigurumi World

Seriously Cute Crochet

ana Paula RímoLi

Martingale®
& C O M P A N Y

Amigurumi World:
Seriously Cute Crochet
© 2008 by Ana Paula Rímoli

Martingale®
& COMPANY

Martingale & Company®
20205 144th Ave. NE
Woodinville, WA
98072-8478 USA
www.martingale-pub.com

Printed in China
13 12 11 10 09 08   8 7 6 5 4 3

Library of Congress Cataloging-in-Publication Data
Library of Congress Control Number: 2007041240

ISBN: 978-1-56477-847-5

MISSION STATEMENT
*Dedicated to providing quality products
and service to inspire creativity.*

CREDITS

President & CEO: Tom Wierzbicki

Publisher: Jane Hamada

Editorial Director: Mary V. Green

Managing Editor: Tina Cook

Developmental Editor: Karen Costello Soltys

Technical Editor: Ursula Reikes

Copy Editor: Kathleen Cubley

Design Director: Stan Green

Assistant Design Director: Regina Girard

Illustrator: Laurel Strand

Cover & Text Designer: Regina Girard

Photographer: Brent Kane

CONTENTS

INTRODUCTION

I was born in Montevideo, the capital city of Uruguay. I learned to crochet there when I was seven years old, and I've been crocheting for over 20 years. Once my daughters, Oli and Martina, were born, I lost patience (and no longer had time) for long, elaborate projects, so I started making little toys for them instead. Searching the Internet, I discovered amazing pictures of amigurumi, which is roughly translated from Japanese as "knitted stuffed toy."

The little toys were extremely cute and I wanted to make some, but I couldn't find any patterns in English— so I started making my own. A couple of toys later, I was totally hooked and couldn't stop. I'm sure you'll find making these little creatures as addictive and fun as I have.

Most of the "amis" (as they're affectionately called) in the book can be finished in a couple of hours and make great presents for kids and grown-ups alike (lots of people are now collecting them). Amigurumi are crocheted in the round, mainly using a simple crochet stitch, and they're easy and fun. After you make a couple of toys, you'll be designing your own in no time!

HAPPY, HAPPY CROCHETING!
~ana

*A few basic tools and simple crochet skills are
all you need to make these delightful amigurumi.*

YARN

All of the toys in this book are crocheted using worsted-weight yarn and a size G/6 (4 mm) crochet hook for the larger toys and a size F/5 (3.75 mm) or E/4 (3.5 mm) hook for the smaller toys. A list of the yarn brands I used for the samples in the book can be found on page 79, but it doesn't really matter which brand you use.

Making amigurumi is a great way to use up all your leftover yarn. Choose colors similar to mine, or be creative and come up with your own color combinations!

People often ask how many toys you can make from one 100-gram skein of worsted-weight yarn. While it varies, depending on the pattern and how tightly you crochet, I can usually get two to three sets of the larger animals, and many, many small toys from just one 100-gram skein of main color. Of course you'll need other colors for some body parts and embellishments.

GAUGE, TENSION, AND HOOK SIZES

The measurements given for each toy are approximate and based on the way I crochet. I crochet pretty tightly, and my gauge is as follows:

4 sts and 5 rows = 1" with G hook and worsted-weight yarn

5 sts and 6 rows = 1" with F hook and worsted-weight yarn

The finished toy size, however, isn't really that important, so don't worry if your gauge is different than mine. Depending on your tension and the yarn you use, your toys might end up being a little bit smaller or larger than the ones I made. Changing to a bigger or smaller hook will give you a bigger or smaller toy, respectively.

STITCHES

Simple stitches are used for these amigurumi projects, which make them perfect for beginners.

Chain (ch): Make a slipknot and place it on the hook. YO, draw the yarn through the slip knot, letting the slip knot slide off the hook. *YO, draw the yarn through the new loop, letting the loop slide off the hook. Repeat from * for the desired number of chains.

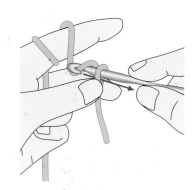

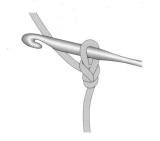

Slip Stitch (sl st): A slip stitch is used to move across one or more stitches. Insert the hook into the stitch, yarn over the hook, and pull through both stitches at once.

Single Crochet (sc): *Insert the hook into the chain or stitch indicated, yarn over the hook, and pull through the chain or stitch (two loops remain on hook).

Yarn over the hook and pull through the remaining two loops on the hook. Repeat from * for the required number of stitches.

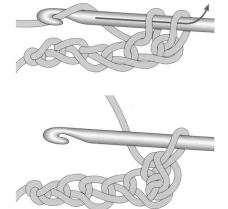

Back post single crochet (BPsc): Insert the hook from the back around the vertical section, or post, of the single crochet stitch in the previous row, and complete the single crochet stitch as usual. Repeat as directed to a get nice, slightly raised, braidlike row of stitches.

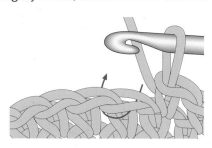

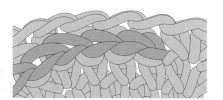

Single Crochet Increase: Work two single crochet stitches into the same stitch.

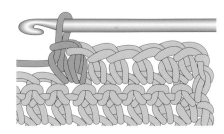

Single Crochet Decrease (dec): (Insert hook into the next stitch, yarn over, pull up a loop) twice; yarn over and pull through all three loops on the hook.

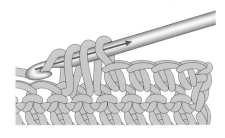

Half Double Crochet (hdc): *Yarn over the hook, insert hook into chain or stitch indicated. Yarn over the hook and pull through the stitch (three loops remain on hook).

Yarn over the hook and pull through all three loops on hook. Rep from * for the required number of stitches.

Double Crochet (dc): *Yarn over the hook, insert hook into chain or stitch indicated. Yarn over the hook and pull through the stitch (three loops are on hook); yarn over the hook and pull through two loops on hook (two loops remain on hook).

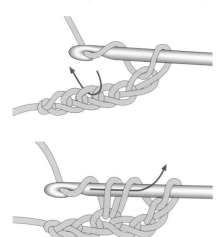

Yarn over the hook and pull through the remaining two loops on hook (one loop remains on hook). Rep from * for the required number of stitches.

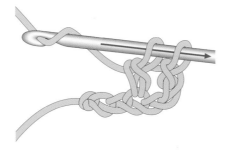

Triple Crochet (tr): *Yarn over the hook twice, insert hook into chain or stitch indicated. *Yarn over the hook and pull through the stitch (four loops on hook); yarn over the hook and pull through two loops on the hook (three loops remain on hook).

(Yarn over the hook and pull through two loops on hook) twice (one loop remains on hook). Repeat from * for the required number of stitches.

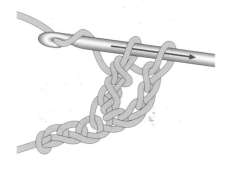

WORKING IN LOOPS

The majority of the stitches are worked in both loops of the stitches from the previous row. There are a few projects where you will work a row into the back loop or the front loop of the stitch.

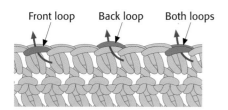

Front loop   Back loop   Both loops

CROCHETING IN THE ROUND

When crocheting in the round, I crochet around and around, forming a continuous spiral. To keep track of where the rounds begin and end you can mark the end or beginning of a round with a safety pin, stitch marker, or little piece of yarn pulled through one of the stitches. At the end of the last round, slip stitch in the first single crochet of the previous round and fasten yarn off.

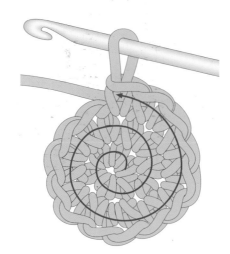

ADDING FACES

Although I have used plastic eyes with safety backings on all of the toys, you can instead embroider the eyes, use buttons, or cut out and sew on little pieces of felt. For each pattern, eye sizes are given in millimeters.

SAFETY

Plastic eyes with safety backings are pretty impossible to take out. I would not, however, give a toy with plastic eyes (or buttons) to a child younger than three years old. Cut-out felt eyes or embroidered eyes are a better choice for young children.

The templates for the muzzles and any other pieces to be cut from felt are included with each project. Cut the felt pieces with sharp scissors to get nice, smooth edges. Using embroidery floss and a needle, I use simple stitches to "draw" the faces on the felt before attaching the felt pieces to the face. To insert plastic eyes in a felt circle, cut a small slit in the felt, just enough to push the stem of the eye through. For very small felt pieces around an eye, you don't need to sew the felt to the face, because the felt will be secured by the eye itself. Sew pieces of felt on with a sharp needle and matching sewing thread, using a very small running stitch close to the edge of the piece.

Mouths: For a simple mouth, bring the needle out at point A, insert needle at point B, leaving a loose strand of yarn to form the mouth. Once you're happy with the shape of the mouth, bring the needle out again at point C, cross over the loose strand of yarn, and insert the needle at point D to make a tiny stitch. Secure ends on wrong side.

For a satin stitch mouth (as seen on Baby Octopus and her Mommy), make a simple mouth as shown below. Then work a very small satin stitch around the curve of the mouth, working the stitches very close together. Make sure to catch a piece of yarn from the face every so often to keep the mouth in place.

Satin stitch noses and eyes: Bring needle out through point A, insert in point B, and repeat, following the shape you want for the nose or eyes and making sure to work stitches really close together. Secure ends on wrong side.

Another option for embroidering a nose is to work from a center point upward. Bring the needle up from underneath at point A; insert the needle at point B. Bring the needle up at point C, very close to point A. Insert the needle back into point B. Continue working stitches close to each other to create a triangle, making sure to always insert the needle back into point B. When you are satisfied with the triangle, make two long stitches across the top of the nose to help define it.

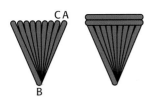

STUFFING

Stuff your toys firmly so they retain their shape and don't look too "droopy." Be careful not to overstuff them, though, because the stuffing will stretch the fabric and may show through the stitches.

I always use polyester fiberfill stuffing because it's nonallergenic, won't bunch up, and it's washable, which is always good when you're making toys! If you do wash the toys, make sure you follow the yarn care instructions on the label.

JOINING THE EXTREMITIES

I always use a tapestry needle and the same color yarn as the pieces (or at least one of the pieces) that I want to join together. When sewing pieces to the body, make sure they are securely attached so that little fingers can't pull them off.

On some animals the opening of the extremities will remain open for sewing onto the body; the instructions will tell you when to leave them open. Position the piece on the body and sew all around it, going through the front stitches of both the extremity and the body.

On other animals, the opening of the extremities will be sewn closed before being attached to the body. To do this, pinch the opening closed, line up the stitches of one side with the other side, and sew through the front loop of one side and the back loop of the other side. Position the piece where you want it on the body and sew.

*	repeat directions between * and * as many times as indicated
BPsc	back post single crochet
ch	chain
dc	double crochet
dec	decrease (see "Single Crochet Decrease" on page 10)
hdc	half double crochet
R	round(s)
rem	remaining

rep	repeat
rnd	round
sc	single crochet
sk	skip
sl st	slip st
st(s)	stitch(es)
tog	together
tr	triple crochet

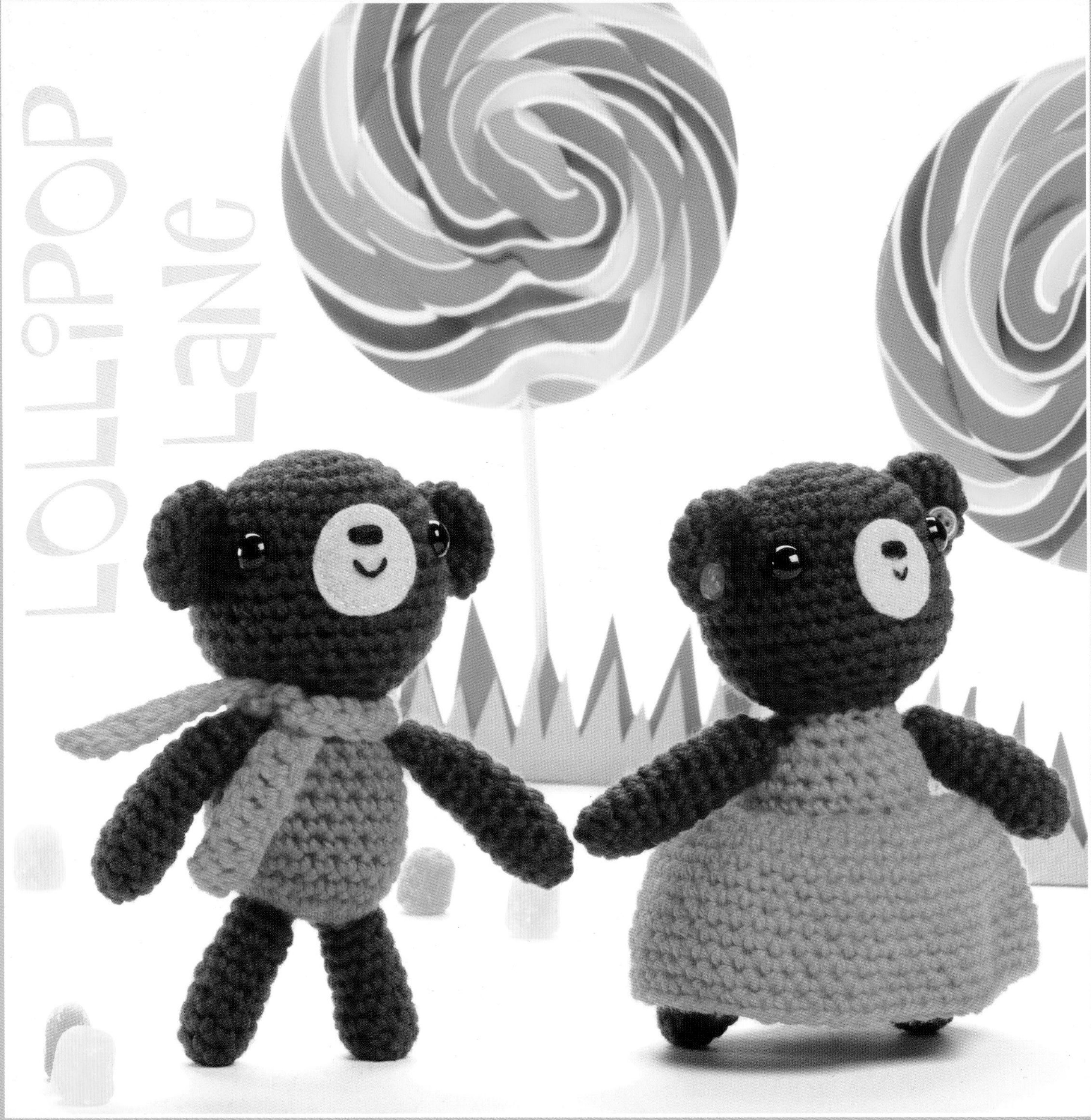
LOLLiPOP
LaNE

Everybody needs a little teddy bear (or two).
Valentino and Valentina are the perfect size;
they are super fast to make and the
sweetest little pair to give as a present.

FINISHED SIZES

Girl and boy bears: Approx 5½"/14 cm tall
Depending on your tension and yarn choice, finished sizes may vary.

MATERIALS

Worsted-weight yarn in brown, pink, red, and white
Size G/6 (4 mm) crochet hook
9 mm plastic eyes with safety backings
Small piece of tan craft felt
Sewing thread and sharp needle
Black embroidery floss and tapestry needle
Fiberfill or stuffing of your choice
Small beads or buttons for earrings

GIRL OR BOY BEAR

HEAD

Using brown yarn,

R1: Ch 2, 6 sc in second chain from hook.

R2: 2 sc in each sc around. (12 sts)

R3: *Sc 1, 2 sc in next sc*, rep 6 times. (18 sts)

R4: *Sc 2, 2 sc in next sc*, rep 6 times. (24 sts)

R5: *Sc 3, 2 sc in next sc*, rep 6 times. (30 sts)

R6–13: Sc 30.

R14: *Sc 3, dec 1*, rep 6 times. (24 sts)

R15: *Sc 2, dec 1*, rep 6 times. (18 sts)

Work on face: Attach eyes. Cut muzzle from felt and embroider nose and mouth. Sew muzzle to head.

R16: Sc 18.

Stuff almost to the top.

R17: *Sc 1, dec 1*, rep 6 times. (12 sts)

Finish stuffing.

Fasten off and weave in loose ends.

EARS (Make 2)

Using brown yarn,

R1: Ch 2, 6 sc in second chain from hook.

R2: 2 sc in each sc around. (12 sts)

R3–4: Sc 12.

Fasten off, leaving a long tail for sewing, and sew to head.

Sew little buttons or beads to Valentina's ears for earrings.

BODY

Start with red yarn if making Valentino and with white yarn (underwear) if making Valentina.

R1: Ch 2, 6 sc in second chain from hook.

R2: 2 sc in each sc around. (12 sts)

R3: *Sc 1, 2 sc in next sc*, rep 6 times. (18 sts)

R4: *Sc 2, 2 sc in next sc*, rep 6 times. (24 sts)

R5–8: Sc 24.

For girl:

R9: Change to skirt color, sc 24.

R10: Sc 24 through back loops only (you'll use the front loops later when crocheting the skirt).

R11: Sc 24.

For boy:

R9–11: Sc 24.

For both:

R12: *Sc 2, dec 1*, rep 6 times. (18 sts)

R13: Sc 18.

Fasten off, leaving a long tail for sewing. Stuff and sew to head.

ARMS AND LEGS (Make 2 of each)

Using brown yarn,

R1: Ch 2, 8 sc in second chain from hook.

R2: Sc 8.

For arms: Rep R2 another 7 times. Fasten off, leaving a long tail for sewing. Stuff, sew open end tog, and sew to body.

For legs: Rep R2 another 5 times. Fasten off, leaving a long tail for sewing. Stuff and sew to body.

SKIRT FOR GIRL

Using pink yarn,

Holding the bear upside down (legs up in the air), join yarn at back of body to one of the front loops you left in R10 of the body.

R1: Sc 24 through front loops all around the body.

R2: 2 sc in each sc around. (48 sts)

R3: Sc 48.

Rep R3 until you're happy with the skirt length.

Fasten off and weave in ends.

SCARF FOR BOY

Using pink yarn,

Loosely ch 40, turn.

Ch 2, hdc in third ch from hook and in each ch across.

Fasten off and weave in ends.

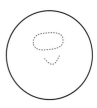

Bear muzzle

When I was little, my cousins and I used to go to a small zoo in the countryside where a single lion was kept in the saddest cage. He would stand on his hind legs, jump on the bars, roar, and scare us silly. I always thought he was so sad all by himself in that horrible place. All these years later, I still think about him once in a while, and I just had to make him a friend and imagine him all happiness and smiles.

FINISHED SIZES

Daddy: Approx 7½"/19 cm tall
Baby: Approx 4"/10 cm tall
Depending on your tension and yarn choice, finished sizes may vary.

MATERIALS

Worsted-weight yarn in gold and orange
Size G/6 (4 mm) and E/4 (3.50 mm) crochet hooks
6 mm and 9 mm plastic eyes with safety backings
Small piece of tan craft felt
Sewing thread and sharp needle
Brown embroidery floss and tapestry needle
Fiberfill or stuffing of your choice

DaDDY

Use gold yarn for everything except the mane and the tip of the tail.

HEAD

Using G hook,

R1: Ch 2, 6 sc in second ch from hook.

R2: 2 sc in each sc around. (12 sts)

R3: *Sc 1, 2 sc in next sc*, rep 6 times. (18 sts)

R4: *Sc 2, 2 sc in next sc*, rep 6 times. (24 sts)

R5: *Sc 3, 2 sc in next sc*, rep 6 times. (30 sts)

R6: *Sc 4, 2 sc in next sc*, rep 6 times. (36 sts)

R7: *Sc 5, 2 sc in next sc*, rep 6 times. (42 sts)

R8–19: Sc 42.

R20: *Sc 5, dec 1*, rep 6 times. (36 sts)

R21: *Sc 4, dec 1*, rep 6 times. (30 sts)

Work on face: Attach eyes. Cut muzzle from felt, embroider nose and mouth, and sew muzzle to head.

R22: *Sc 3, dec 1*, rep 6 times. (24 sts)

R23: *Sc 2, dec 1*, rep 6 times. (18 sts)

R24: *Sc 1, dec 1*, rep 6 times. (12 sts)

Stuff head.

R25: *Sk 1 sc, sc 1*, rep 6 times. (6 sts)

Fasten off and weave in ends.

MANE

Using G hook and orange yarn,

Loosely ch 45.

4 tr in fourth ch from hook, sk 1 sc, sl st 1, *5 tr in next st, sk 1 sc, sl st 1, rep from * 13 times.

Fasten off, leaving a long tail for sewing. Sew both ends tog and place mane on lion's head as if it were a headband. When you're happy with the position of the mane, sew it in place.

EARS (Make 2)

Using G hook,

R1: Ch 2, 5 sc in second ch from hook.

R2: 2 sc in each sc around. (10 sts)

R3: Sc 10.

Fasten off, leaving a long tail for sewing, and sew to head in front of mane.

BODY

Using G hook,

R1: Ch 2, 6 sc in second ch from hook.

R2: 2 sc in each sc around. (12 sts)

R3: *Sc 1, 2 sc in next sc*, rep 6 times. (18 sts)

R4: *Sc 2, 2 sc in next sc*, rep 6 times. (24 sts)

R5–14: Sc 24.

R15: *Sc 2, dec 1*, rep 6 times. (18 sts)

R16 and 17: Sc 18.

Fasten off, leaving a long tail for sewing. Stuff and sew to head.

LEGS AND ARMS (Make 2 of each)

Using G hook,

R1: Ch 2, 5 sc in second ch from hook.

R2: 2 sc in each sc around. (10 sts)

Arms: R3–15: Sc 10.

Fasten off, leaving a long tail for sewing. Stuff, sew open end tog, and sew arm to body.

Legs: R3–12: Sc 10.

Fasten off, leaving a long tail for sewing. Stuff, sew open end tog, and sew leg to body.

TAIL

Using G hook and orange yarn,

R1: Ch 2, 6 sc in second ch from hook.

R2: Sc 6.

R3: 2 sc in each sc around. (12 sts)

R4: *Sk 1 sc, sc 1*, rep 6 times. (6 sts)

Stuff end a little and change to gold yarn.

R5: Sc 6.

Rep R5 until tail is approx 3½"/9 cm long.

Fasten off, leaving a long tail for sewing, and sew to body.

PUPPY

NOSE

Using black yarn,

R1: Ch 2, 5 sc in second ch from hook.

R2: 2 sc in each sc around. (10 sts)

Fasten off, leaving a long tail for sewing, and set aside.

EYE SPOT

Using orange yarn,

R1: Ch 2, 5 sc in second ch from hook.

R2: 2 sc in each sc around. (10 sts)

Fasten off, leaving a long tail for sewing, and set aside.

HEAD

Using brown yarn,

R1: Ch 2, 5 sc in second ch from hook.

R2: 2 sc in each sc around. (10 sts)

R3: *Sc 1, 2 sc in next sc*, rep 5 times. (15 sts)

R4: *Sc 2, 2 sc in next sc*, rep 5 times. (20 sts)

R5: *Sc 3, 2 sc in next sc*, rep 5 times. (25 sts)

R6–13: Sc 25.

Work on face: Insert one eye into center of eye spot, attach eye to head, and sew spot to head. Attach second eye to head. Sew nose on head.

R14: *Sc 3, dec 1*, rep 5 times. (20 sts)

R15–17: Sc 20.

R18: *Sc 2, dec 1*, rep 5 times. (15 sts)

Stuff head almost to the top.

R19: *Sc 1, dec 1*, rep 5 times. (10 sts)

Finish stuffing.

R20: *Sk 1 sc, sc 1*, rep 5 times. (5 sts)

Fasten off and weave in ends.

EARS (Make 2)

Using brown yarn,

R1: Ch 2, 4 sc in second ch from hook.

R2: 2 sc in each sc around. (8 sts)

R3–7: Sc 8.

Fasten off, leaving a long tail for sewing. Stuff and sew to head.

BODY

Using brown yarn,

R1: Ch 2, 5 sc in second ch from hook.

R2: 2 sc in each sc around. (10 sts)

R3: *Sc 1, 2 sc in next sc*, rep 5 times. (15 sts)

R4: *Sc 2, 2 sc in next sc*, rep 5 times. (20 sts)

R5–8: Sc 20.

R9: *Sc 2, dec 1*, rep 5 times. (15 sts)

R10–13: Sc 15.

Fasten off, leaving a long tail for sewing. Stuff and sew to head.

LEGS (Make 4)

Using brown yarn,

R1: Ch 2, 4 sc in second ch from hook.

R2: 2 sc in each sc around. (8 sts)

R3–6: Sc 8.

Fasten off, leaving a long tail for sewing. Stuff and sew to body.

Make 1 leg a different color if desired.

TAIL

Using orange yarn,

R1: Ch 2, 4 sc in second ch from hook.

R2 and 3: Sc 4.

Fasten off, leaving a long tail for sewing, and sew to body. No need to stuff tail.

BaBY MONKEY aND HER DaDDY

*Who doesn't love monkeys? They're fun, playful, and cute—
and lots of fun to crochet, too! Make Daddy and Baby Monkey,
and your little monkeys will jump around in joy. Just make
sure they don't jump on the bed—they might bump their heads! To
make Mommy monkey, add a skirt and earrings to the Daddy pattern.*

FiNiSHeD SiZeS

Daddy: Approx. 10"/25.5 cm tall
Baby: Approx 6"/15 cm tall
Depending on your tension and yarn choice, finished sizes may vary.

MaTeRiaLS

Worsted-weight yarn in brown and red
Size G/6 (4mm) crochet hook
9 mm plastic eyes with safety backings
Small piece of tan craft felt
Sewing thread and sharp needle
Brown embroidery floss and tapestry needle
Fiberfill or stuffing of your choice
2 little buttons or beads for earrings (4 buttons if making Mommy)

DaDDY

HEAD

Using brown yarn,

R1: Ch 2, 6 sc in second ch from hook.

R2: 2 sc in each sc around. (12 sts)

R3: *Sc 1, 2 sc in next sc*, rep 6 times. (18 sts)

R4: *Sc 2, 2 sc in next sc*, rep 6 times. (24 sts)

R5: *Sc 3, 2 sc in next sc*, rep 6 times. (30 sts)

R6: *Sc 4, 2 sc in next sc*, rep 6 times. (36 sts)

R7: *Sc 5, 2 sc in next sc*, rep 6 times. (42 sts)

R8–19: Sc 42.

R20: *Sc 5, dec 1*, rep 6 times. (36 sts)

R21: *Sc 4, dec 1*, rep 6 times. (30 sts)

Work on face: Cut out muzzle and eye pieces from felt. Embroider nose and mouth on muzzle and sew to head. Cut a little slit in middle of eye pieces, put eyes through slit, and sew felt pieces to head.

R22: Sc 30.

R23: *Sc 3, dec 1*, rep 6 times. (24 sts)

R24: *Sc 2, dec 1*, rep 6 times. (18 sts)

R25: *Sc 1, dec 1*, rep 6 times. (12 sts)

Stuff head.

R26: *Sk 1 sc, sc 1*, rep 6 times. (6 sts)

Fasten off and weave in ends.

EARS (Make 2)

Using brown yarn,

R1: Ch 2, 6 sc in second ch from hook.

R2: 2 sc in each sc around. (12 sts)

R3–5: Sc 12.

Fasten off, leaving a long tail for sewing, and sew to head.

BODY

Using brown yarn,

R1: Ch 2, 6 sc in second ch from hook.

R2: 2 sc in each sc around. (12 sts)

R3: *Sc 1, 2 sc in next sc*, rep 6 times. (18 sts)

R4: *Sc 2, 2 sc in next sc*, rep 6 times. (24 sts)

R5: *Sc 3, 2 sc in next sc*, rep 6 times. (30 sts)

R6–11: Sc 30.

Change to red yarn.

For Daddy:

R12: Sc 30.

R13: BPsc 30.

If making Mommy:

R12: Sc 30 through back loops only (you'll use the front loops later when crocheting the skirt).

R13: Sc 30.

For both:

R14–20: Sc 30.

R21: *Sc 3, dec 1*, rep 6 times. (24 sts)

R22: Sc 24.

R23: *Sc 2, dec 1*, rep 6 times. (18 sts)

R24: Sc 18.

Stuff body.

Fasten off, leaving a long tail for sewing, and sew to head.

ARMS (Make 2)

Using brown yarn,

R1: Ch 2, 6 sc in second ch from hook.

R2: 2 sc in each sc around. (12 sts)

R3–23: Sc 12, stuffing as you go.

Change to red yarn.

R24: Sc 12.

R25: BPsc 12.

R26–35: Sc 12, stuffing as you go.

Fasten off, leaving a long tail for sewing. Sew open end tog and sew to body.

LEGS (Make 2)

Using brown yarn,

R1: Ch 2, 6 sc in second ch from hook.

R2: 2 sc in each sc around. (12 sts)

R3–17: Sc 12, stuffing as you go.

Fasten off, leaving a long tail for sewing, and sew to body.

TAIL

Using brown yarn,

R1: Ch 2, 8 sc in second ch from hook.

R2: Sc 8.

Rep R2, stuffing as you go, until tail is approx 6"/15 cm long.

Fasten off, leaving a long tail for sewing, and sew to body.

SKIRT FOR MOMMY (optional)

Using red yarn,

Holding doll upside down (legs up in the air), join yarn at back of body to one of the front loops you left in R12 when making body.

R1: Sc 30 through front loops all around body.

R2: 2 sc in each sc around. (60 sts)

R3: Sc 60.

Rep R3 until you're happy with the skirt length.

Fasten off and weave in ends.

R15: *Sc 3, dec 1*, rep 6 times. (24 sts)

R16: Sc 24.

R17: *Sc 2, dec 1*, rep 6 times. (18 sts)

R18: *Sc 1, dec 1*, rep 6 times. (12 sts)

Stuff head.

R19: *Sk 1 sc, sc 1*, rep 6 times. (6 sts)

Fasten off and weave in ends.

EARS (Make 2)

Using brown yarn,

R1: Ch 2, 5 sc in second ch from hook.

R2: 2 sc in each sc around. (10 sts)

R3 and 4: Sc 10.

Fasten off, leaving a long tail for sewing.
Sew little buttons or beads to ear
lobes and sew ears to head.

BODY

Using brown yarn,

R1: Ch 2, 6 sc in second ch from hook.

R2: 2 sc in each sc around. (12 sts)

R3: *Sc 1, 2 sc in next sc*, rep 6
times. (18 sts)

R4: *Sc 2, 2 sc in next sc*, rep 6
times. (24 sts)

R5 and 6: Sc 24.

Change to red yarn.

For girl:

R7: Sc 24 through back loops only
(you'll use the front loops later when
crocheting the skirt)

R8: Sc 24.

BaBY

HEAD

Using brown yarn,

R1: Ch 2, 6 sc in second ch from hook.

R2: 2 sc in each sc around. (12 sts)

R3: *Sc 1, 2 sc in next sc*, rep 6
times. (18 sts)

R4: *Sc 2, 2 sc in next sc*, rep 6
times. (24 sts)

R5: *Sc 3, 2 sc in next sc*, rep 6
times. (30 sts)

R6–14: Sc 30.

Work on face: Cut out muzzle and eye
pieces from felt. Embroider nose
and mouth on muzzle and sew to
head. Cut a little slit in middle of eye
pieces, put eyes through slit, and
sew felt pieces to head.

For boy:

R7: Sc 24.

R8: BPsc 24.

For both:

R9–11: Sc 24.

R12: *Sc 2, dec 1*, rep 6 times. (18 sts)

R13: Sc 18.

Stuff body.

Fasten off, leaving a long tail for sewing, and sew to head.

ARMS (Make 2)

Using brown yarn,

R1: Ch 2, 4 sc in second ch from hook.

R2: 2 sc in each sc around. (8 sts)

R3–7: Sc 8, stuffing as you go.

Change to red yarn.

R8: Sc 8.

R9: BPsc 8.

R10–19: Sc 8, stuffing as you go.

Fasten off, leaving a long tail for sewing. Sew open end tog and sew to body.

LEGS (Make 2)

Using brown yarn,

R1: Ch 2, 4 sc in second ch from hook.

R2: 2 sc in each sc around. (8 sts)

R3–9: Sc 8, stuffing as you go.

Fasten off, leaving a long tail for sewing, and sew to body.

TAIL

Using brown yarn,

R1: Ch 2, 5 sc in second ch from hook.

R2: Sc 5.

Rep R2, stuffing as you go, until tail is approx 2½"/6 cm long.

Fasten off, leaving a long tail for sewing, and sew to body.

SKIRT

Using red yarn,

Holding doll upside down (legs up in the air), join yarn at back of body to one of front loops you left in R7 when making body.

R1: Sc 24 through front loops all around body.

R2: 2 sc in each sc around. (48 sts)

R3: Sc 48.

Rep R3 until you're happy with the skirt length. Fasten off and weave in ends.

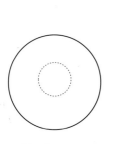

Monkey eye

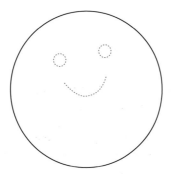

Daddy monkey muzzle

Baby monkey muzzle

STAYING COOL

BABY PENGUIN AND HER MOMMY

Between watching March of the Penguins *and* Happy Feet, *my daughter Oli won't stop talking about and walking like a little penguin, so I had to make some.*

FINISHED SIZES

Mommy: Approx 6½"/16.5 cm tall
Baby: Approx 4½"/11.5 cm tall
Depending on your tension and yarn choice, finished sizes may vary.

MATERIALS

Worsted-weight yarn in black, blue, yellow, and white
Size G/6 (4 mm) and F/5 (3.75 mm) crochet hooks
9 mm plastic eyes with safety backings
Fiberfill or stuffing of your choice

HEAD

Using G hook and black yarn,

R1: Ch 2, 6 sc in second ch from hook.

R2: 2 sc in each sc around. (12 sts)

R3: *Sc 1, 2 sc in next sc*, rep 6 times. (18 sts)

R4: *Sc 2, 2 sc in next sc*, rep 6 times. (24 sts)

R5: *Sc 3, 2 sc in next sc*, rep 6 times. (30 sts)

R6: *Sc 4, 2 sc in next sc*, rep 6 times. (36 sts)

R7: *Sc 5, 2 sc in next sc*, rep 6 times. (42 sts)

R8–19: Sc 42.

R20: *Sc 5, dec 1*, rep 6 times. (36 sts)

R21: *Sc 4, dec 1*, rep 6 times. (30 sts)

Work on face: Insert eyes into roundies, attach eyes to head, and sew roundies to head. Stuff beak and sew to head.

R22: Sc 30.

R23: *Sc 3, dec 1*, rep 6 times. (24 sts)

R24: *Sc 2, dec 1*, rep 6 times. (18 sts)

Stuff head firmly.

R25: *Sc 1, dec 1*, rep 6 times. (12 sts)

Fasten off and weave in ends.

MOMMY

EYE ROUNDIES (Make 2)

Using F hook and blue yarn,

R1: Ch 2, 6 sc in second ch from hook.

R2: 2 sc in each sc around. (12 sts)

R3: *Sc 1, 2 sc in next sc*, rep 6 times. (18 sts)

Fasten off, leaving a long tail for sewing, and set aside.

BEAK

Using F hook and yellow yarn,

R1: Ch 2, 5 sc in second ch from hook.

R2: 2 sc in each sc around. (10 sts)

R3: Sc 10.

R4: *Sc 1, 2 sc in next sc*, rep 5 times. (15 sts)

R5 and 6: Sc 15.

Fasten off, leaving a long tail for sewing, and set aside.

BELLY SPOT

Using G hook and white yarn,

R1: Ch 2, 6 sc in second ch from hook.

R2: 2 sc in each sc around. (12 sts)

R3: *Sc 1, 2 sc in next sc*, rep 6 times. (18 sts)

R4: *4 sc in next sc, sc 8*, rep twice. (24 sts)

R5: *Dc 4, hdc 8*, rep twice. (24 sts)

Fasten off, leaving a long tail for sewing, and set aside.

BODY

Using G hook and black yarn,

R1: Ch 2, 6 sc in second ch from hook.

R2: 2 sc in each sc around. (12 sts)

R3: *Sc 1, 2 sc in next sc*, rep 6 times. (18 sts)

R4: *Sc 2, 2 sc in next sc*, rep 6 times. (24 sts)

R5: *Sc 3, 2 sc in next sc*, rep 6 times. (30 sts)

R6: *Sc 4, 2 sc in next sc*, rep 6 times. (36 sts)

R7: *Sc 5, 2 sc in next sc*, rep 6 times. (42 sts)

R8: *Sc 6, 2 sc in next sc*, rep 6 times. (48 sts)

R9–14: Sc 48.

R15: *Sc 6, dec 1*, rep 6 times. (42 sts)

R16: Sc 42.

R17: *Sc 5, dec 1*, rep 6 times. (36 sts)

R18–20: Sc 36.

R21: *Sc 4, dec 1*, rep 6 times. (30 sts)

R22–25: Sc 30.

R26: *Sc 3, dec 1*, rep 6 times. (24 sts)

R27: Sc 24.

Fasten off, leaving a long tail for sewing. Sew belly spot to body, stuff body firmly, and sew to head.

FEET (Make 2)

Using G hook and yellow yarn,

R1: Ch 2, 8 sc in second ch from hook.

R2: 2 sc in each sc around. (16 sts)

R3–8: Sc 16.

Fasten off, leaving a long tail for sewing. Stuff, sew open end tog, and sew to body. Make sure you sew feet almost to edge of body so your penguin can stand by herself.

WINGS (Make 2)

Using G hook and black yarn,

R1: Ch 2, 7 sc in second ch from hook.

R2: 2 sc in each sc around. (14 sts)

R3–13: Sc 14.

R14: *Sk 1 sc, sc 1*, rep 7 times. (7 sts)

Fasten off, leaving a long tail for sewing. Sew open end tog and sew to body (no need to stuff wings).

BaBY

EYE ROUNDIES (Make 2)

Using F hook and blue yarn,

R1: Ch 2, 6 sc in second ch from hook.

R2: 2 sc in each sc around. (12 sts)

Fasten off, leaving a long tail for sewing, and set aside.

BEAK

Using F hook and yellow yarn,

R1: Ch 2, 4 sc in second ch from hook.

R2: 2 sc in each sc around. (8 sts)

R3: Sc 8.

R4: *Sc 1, 2 sc in next sc*, rep 4 times. (12 sts)

R5: Sc 12.

Fasten off, leaving a long tail for sewing, and set aside.

HEAD

Using G hook and black yarn,

R1: Ch 2, 6 sc in second ch from hook.

R2: 2 sc in each sc around. (12 sts)

R3: *Sc 1, 2 sc in next sc*, rep 6 times. (18 sts)

R4: *Sc 2, 2 sc in next sc*, rep 6 times. (24 sts)

R5: *Sc 3, 2 sc in next sc*, rep 6 times. (30 sts)

R6–14: Sc 30.

R15: *Sc 3, dec 1*, rep 6 times. (24 sts)

Work on face: Insert eyes into roundies, attach eyes to head, and sew roundies to head. Stuff beak and sew to head.

R16: *Sc 2, dec 1*, rep 6 times. (18 sts)

R17: Sc 18.

Stuff head firmly.

R18: *Sc 1, dec 1*, rep 6 times. (12 sts)

Fasten off and weave in ends.

BELLY SPOT

Using G hook and white yarn,

R1: Ch 2, 6 sc in second ch from hook.

R2: 2 sc in each sc around. (12 sts)

R3: *3 sc in next sc, sc 5*, rep twice. (16 sts)

Fasten off, leaving a long tail for sewing, and set aside.

BODY

Using G hook and black yarn,

R1: Ch 2, 6 sc in second ch from hook.

R2: 2 sc in each sc around. (12 sts)

R3: *Sc 1, 2 sc in next sc*, rep 6 times. (18 sts)

R4: *Sc 2, 2 sc in next sc*, rep 6 times. (24 sts)

R5: *Sc 3, 2 sc in next sc*, rep 6 times. (30 sts)

R6: *Sc 4, 2 sc in next sc*, rep 6 times. (36 sts)

R7–9: Sc 36.

R10: *Sc 4, dec 1*, rep 6 times. (30 sts)

R11: *Sc 3, dec 1*, rep 6 times. (24 sts)

R12: *Sc 2, dec 1*, rep 6 times. (18 sts)

R13–15: Sc 18.

Fasten off, leaving a long tail for sewing. Sew belly spot to body, stuff body firmly, and sew to head.

FEET (Make 2)

Using G hook and yellow yarn,

R1: Ch 2, 5 sc in second ch from hook.

R2: 2 sc in each sc around. (10 sts)

R3–5: Sc 10.

Fasten off, leaving a long tail for sewing. Stuff, sew open end tog, and sew to body. Make sure you sew feet almost to the edge of body so your penguin can stand by herself.

WINGS (Make 2)

Using G hook and black yarn,

R1: Ch 2, 4 sc in second ch from hook.

R2: 2 sc in each sc around. (8 sts)

R3–9: Sc 8.

Fasten off, leaving a long tail for sewing. Sew open end tog and sew to body (no need to stuff wings).

MOMMY

EYE ROUNDIES (Make 2)

Using gold yarn,

R1: Ch 3, 6 hdc in third ch from hook.

R2: 2 hdc in each hdc around. (12 sts)

R3: *Sc 1, 2 sc in next hdc*, rep 6 times. (18 sts)

Fasten off, leaving a long tail for sewing. Set aside.

BODY

Using brown yarn,

R1: Ch 2, 6 sc in second ch from hook.

R2: 2 sc in each sc around. (12 sts)

R3: *Sc 1, 2 sc in next sc*, rep 6 times. (18 sts)

R4: *Sc 2, 2 sc in next sc*, rep 6 times. (24 sts)

R5: *Sc 3, 2 sc in next sc*, rep 6 times. (30 sts)

R6: *Sc 4, 2 sc in next sc*, rep 6 times. (36 sts)

R7–12: Sc 36.

Change to tan yarn.

R13–18: Sc 36.

Work on face: Insert eyes into roundies, attach eyes to head, and sew roundies to head. Embroider beak using orange yarn.

R19: *Sc 5, 2 sc in next sc*, rep 6 times. (42 sts)

R20–28: Sc 42.

R29: *Sc 5, dec 1*, rep 6 times. (36 sts)

R30: *Sc 4, dec 1*, rep 6 times. (30 sts)

R31: *Sc 3, dec 1*, rep 6 times. (24 sts)

R32: *Sc 2, dec 1*, rep 6 times. (18 sts)

R33: *Sc 1, dec 1*, rep 6 times. (12 sts)

Stuff body.

R34: *Sk 1 sc, sc 1*, rep 6 times. (6 sts)

Fasten off and weave in ends.

WINGS (Make 2)

Using gold yarn,

R1: Ch 2, 6 sc in second ch from hook.

R2: 2 sc in each sc around. (12 sts)

R3–10: Sc 12.

Fasten off, leaving a long tail for sewing. Sew open end tog and sew to body (no need to stuff wings).

BABY

EYE ROUNDIES (Make 2)

Using gold yarn,

R1: Ch 3, 6 hdc in third ch from hook.

R2: 2 sc in each hdc around. (12 sts)

Fasten off, leaving a long tail for sewing. Set aside.

BODY

Using brown yarn,

R1: Ch 2, 6 sc in second ch from hook.

R2: 2 sc in each sc around. (12 sts)

R3: *Sc 1, 2 sc in next sc*, rep 6 times. (18 sts)

R4: *Sc 2, 2 sc in next sc*, rep 6 times. (24 sts)

R5–8: Sc 24.

Change to tan yarn.

R9–14: Sc 24.

Work on face: Insert eyes into roundies, attach eyes to head, and sew roundies to head. Embroider beak with orange yarn.

R15: *Sc 3, 2 sc in next sc*, rep 6 times. (30 sts)

R16–18: Sc 30.

R19: *Sc 3, dec 1*, rep 6 times. (24 sts)

R20: *Sc 2, dec 1*, rep 6 times. (18 sts)

R21: *Sc 1, dec 1*, rep 6 times. (12 sts)

Stuff body.

R22: *Sk 1 sc, sc 1*, rep 6 times. (6 sts)

Fasten off and weave in ends.

WINGS (Make 2)

Using brown yarn,

R1: Ch 2, 5 sc in second ch from hook.

R2: 2 sc in each sc around. (10 sts)

R3–7: Sc 10.

Fasten off, leaving a long tail for sewing. Sew open end tog and sew to body (no need to stuff wings).

MUSHROOMS &
MUNCHKINS

BABY HEDGEHOG AND HER MOMMY

*Hedgehogs remind me of little babies, all cute and cuddly and shy.
Mine, however, turned out like little disco kids. Don't they
remind you of the '70s, with their hair and carefree look?
Maybe you have a friend who loves the '70s that would like
to have these little cuties as dancing companions.*

FINISHED SIZES

Mommy: Approx 4½"/11.5 cm tall
Baby: Approx 3"/7.5 cm tall
Depending on your tension and yarn choice, finished sizes may vary.

MATERIALS

Worsted-weight yarn in tan and brown
Size G/6 (4 mm) crochet hook
6 mm and 9 mm plastic eyes with safety backings
Black and red embroidery floss and tapestry needle
Fiberfill or stuffing of your choice
2 little mushrooms (optional, available at www.smallstump.com)

MOMMY

MUZZLE

Using tan yarn,

R1: Ch 2, 5 sc in second ch from hook.

R2: 2 sc in each sc around. (10 sts)

R3: *Sc 1, 2 sc in next sc*, rep 5 times. (15 sts)

R4: Sc 15.

Fasten off, leaving a long tail for sewing.

Embroider nose and mouth and set aside.

HEAD AND BODY

Using tan yarn,

R1: Ch 2, 8 sc in second ch from hook.

R2: 2 sc in each sc around. (16 sts)

R3: *Sc 1, 2 sc in next sc*, rep 8 times. (24 sts)

R4: *Sc 2, 2 sc in next sc*, rep 8 times. (32 sts)

R5: *Sc 3, 2 sc in next sc*, rep 8 times. (40 sts)

R6–17: Sc 40.

R18: *Sc 6, dec 1*, rep 5 times. (35 sts)

R19: *Sc 5, dec 1*, rep 5 times. (30 sts)

R20–22: Sc 30.

R23: *Sc 4, dec 1*, rep 5 times. (25 sts)

R24: Sc 25.

R25: *Sc 3, dec 1*, rep 5 times. (20 sts)

Work on face: Sew muzzle in place and attach 9 mm eyes.

R26: *Sc 2, dec 1*, rep 5 times. (15 sts)

Stuff body.

R27: *Sc 1, dec 1*, rep 5 times. (10 sts)

R28: *Sk 1 sc, sc 1*, rep 5 times. (5 sts)

Fasten off and weave in ends.

EARS (Make 2)

Using tan yarn,

Ch 3, 6 dc in third ch from hook.

Fasten off, leaving long tail for sewing.

Fold in half, sew bottom part tog (so ears look like little mouse ears), and sew to head.

PRICKLY COAT

Using brown yarn, join yarn at a sc on bottom of back of body. Get ready; this takes forever!

I worked in rows all over the back and on top of the head as follows:

*Ch 3, sk 2 sc, sc 1, rep from *.

Fasten off and weave in ends.

ARMS (Make 2)

Using tan yarn,

R1: Ch 2, 5 sc in second ch from hook.

R2: 2 sc in each sc around. (10 sts)

R3–8: Sc 10.

Fasten off, leaving long tail for sewing. Stuff lightly and sew to body.

BABY

MUZZLE

Using tan yarn,

R1: Ch 2, 5 sc in second ch from hook.

R2: 2 sc in each sc around. (10 sts)

R3: Sc 10.

Fasten off, leaving a long tail for sewing. Embroider nose and mouth and set aside.

HEAD AND BODY

Using tan yarn,

R1: Ch 2, 8 sc in second ch from hook.

R2: 2 sc in each sc around. (16 sts)

R3: *Sc 1, 2 sc in next sc*, rep 8 times. (24 sts)

R4–10: Sc 24.

R11: *Sc 4, dec 1*, rep 4 times. (20 sts)

R12 and 13: Sc 20.

R14: *Sc 3, dec 1*, rep 4 times. (16 sts)

Work on face: Sew muzzle in place and attach 6 mm eyes.

R15: *Sc 2, dec 1*, rep 4 times. (12 sts)

Stuff body.

R16: *Sc 1, dec 1*, rep 4 times. (8 sts)

R17: *Sk 1 sc, sc 1*, rep 4 times. (4 sts)

Fasten off and weave in ends.

EARS (Make 2)

Using tan yarn,

Ch 2, 7 sc in third ch from hook.

Fasten off, leaving long tail for sewing.

Fold ears in half, sew bottom part tog
(so ears look like little mouse ears),
and sew to head.

PRICKLY COAT

Work as for Mommy.

ARMS (Make 2)

Using tan yarn,

R1: Ch 2, 3 sc in second ch from hook.

R2: 2 sc in each sc around. (6 sts)

R3–6: Sc 6.

Fasten off, leaving long tail for sewing.
Stuff lightly and sew to body.

Villa Dolores is Montevideo's zoo, and for the longest time,
Leo the baby elephant was its most visited and popular resident.
We all drew pictures of him and visited and brought him peanuts.
My drawings always involved a long scarf and a friend with
a tutu, so here's Leo and friend in their softie versions.

FINISHED SIZE

Approx 7"/17.75 cm tall
Depending on your tension and yarn choice, finished sizes may vary.

MATERIALS

Worsted-weight yarn in gray, pink, white, and green
Size G/6 (4 mm) crochet hook
9 mm plastic eyes with safety backings
Small pieces of white craft felt
Sewing thread and sharp needle
Black embroidery floss and tapestry needle
Fiberfill or stuffing of your choice

BOY OR GIRL ELEPHANT

TRUNK

Use gray yarn if making boy and pink yarn if making girl.

R1: Ch 2, 6 sc in second ch from hook.

R2: 2 sc in each sc around. (12 sts)

R3–7: Sc 12.

R8: Hdc 6 through back loops only, sc 6.

R9–12: Sc 12.

R13: *Sc 1, 2 sc in next sc*, rep 6 times. (18 sts)

R14: Sc 18.

Fasten off, leaving a long tail for sewing. Stuff and set aside.

HEAD

R1: Ch 2, 6 sc in second ch from hook.

R2: 2 sc in each sc around. (12 sts)

R3: *Sc 1, 2 sc in next sc*, rep 6 times. (18 sts)

R4: *Sc 2, 2 sc in next sc*, rep 6 times. (24 sts)

R5: *Sc 3, 2 sc in next sc*, rep 6 times. (30 sts)

R6: *Sc 4, 2 sc in next sc*, rep 6 times. (36 sts)

R7: *Sc 5, 2 sc in next sc*, rep 6 times. (42 sts)

R8–18: Sc 42.

Work on face: Sew trunk to head. Cut 2 circles from white felt. Cut a small slit in middle of each circle, insert eyes, and secure to head. Sew circles to head.

R19: *Sc 5, dec 1*, rep 6 times. (36 sts)

R20: *Sc 4, dec 1*, rep 6 times. (30 sts)

R21: Sc 30.

R22: *Sc 3, dec 1*, rep 6 times. (24 sts)

R23: *Sc 2, dec 1*, rep 6 times. (18 sts)

Stuff head firmly.

R24: *Sc 1, dec 1*, rep 6 times. (12 sts)

R25: *Sk 1 sc, sc 1*, rep 6 times. (6 sts)

Fasten off and weave in ends.

EARS (Make 2)

R1: Ch 2, 6 sc in second ch from hook.

R2: 2 sc in each sc around. (12 sts)

R3: *Sc 1, 2 sc in next sc*, rep 6 times. (18 sts)

R4: *Sc 2, 2 sc in next sc*, rep 6 times. (24 sts)

R5–10: Sc 24.

R11: *Sc 2, dec 1*, rep 6 times. (18 sts)

R12: Sc 18.

R13: *Sc 1, dec 1*, rep 6 times. (12 sts)

R14–15: Sc 12.

Fasten off, leaving a long tail for sewing. Sew open end tog and sew to head.

BODY

R1: Ch 2, 6 sc in second ch from hook.

R2: 2 sc in each sc around. (12 sts)

R3: *Sc 1, 2 sc in next sc*, rep 6 times. (18 sts)

R4: *Sc 2, 2 sc in next sc*, rep 6 times. (24 sts)

R5: *Sc 3, 2 sc in next sc*, rep 6 times. (30 sts)

R6–8: Sc 30.

For girl:

R9: Sc 30 through back loops only. (You'll use the front loops later when crocheting the skirt.)

For boy:

R9: Sc 30.

For both:

R10: *Sc 3, dec 1*, rep 6 times. (24 sts)

R11–15: Sc 24.

Fasten off, leaving a long tail for sewing. Stuff and sew to body.

SKIRT FOR GIRL

Using white yarn,

Holding doll upside down (legs up in the air), join yarn at back to one of the front loops you left in R9 when making body.

R1: Sc 30 through the front loops all around body.

R2: Sc 2 in each sc around. (60 sts)

R3: Sc 60.

Rep R3 until you're happy with the skirt length.

Fasten off and weave in ends.

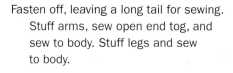

LEGS AND ARMS (Make 2 of each)

R1: Ch 2, 6 sc in second ch from hook.

R2: 2 sc in each sc around. (12 sts)

R3: *Sc 1, 2 sc in next sc*, rep 6 times. (18 sts)

R4: *Sc 2, 2 sc in next sc*, rep 6 times. (24 sts)

R5: Through back loops only, *sc 2, dec 1*, rep 6 times. (18 sts)

R6: *Sc 1, dec 1*, rep 6 times. (12 sts)

R7: Sc 12.

Toenails: Cut 2 toenail pieces from felt. Referring to photo, sew to top of foot.

R8–11: Sc 12.

Fasten off, leaving a long tail for sewing. Stuff arms, sew open end tog, and sew to body. Stuff legs and sew to body.

TAIL

Ch 5. Starting in second ch from hook, sl 1 st, sc 1, hdc 1, dc 1.

Fasten off, leaving long tail for sewing, and sew to body.

SCARF FOR BOY

Using green yarn,

Loosely ch 80, turn.

R1: Ch 2, hdc in third ch from hook and in each ch across.

R2: Hdc 80.

Fasten off and weave in loose ends.

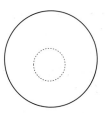

Elephant eye

Elephant toes

The octopi were the first in a moms and babies series I started right after my daughter Martina was born. I figured that with a newborn and a three-year-old I would actually need eight arms to be able to hug them both as many times as I wanted to, and to keep up with the housework—don't we all wish we had eight arms once in awhile?

FINISHED SIZES

Mommy: Approx 3"/7.5 cm when sitting
Baby: Approx 2¼"/5.75 cm when sitting
Depending on your tension and yarn choice, finished sizes may vary.

MATERIALS

Worsted-weight yarn in desired color
Size F/5 (4 mm) crochet hook
9mm plastic eyes with safety backings
Small pieces of red and pink craft felt
Sewing thread and sharp needle
Black embroidery floss and tapestry needle
Fiberfill or stuffing of your choice

MOMMY

HEAD AND BODY

R1: Ch 2, 6 sc in second chain from hook.

R2: 2 sc in each sc around. (12 sts)

R3: *Sc 1, 2 sc in next sc*, rep 6 times. (18 sts)

R4: *Sc 2, 2 sc in next sc*, rep 6 times. (24 sts)

R5: *Sc 3, 2 sc in next sc*, rep 6 times. (30 sts)

R6: *Sc 4, 2 sc in next sc*, rep 6 times. (36 sts)

R7: *Sc 5, 2 sc in next sc*, rep 6 times. (42 sts)

R8–18: Sc 42.

R19: *Sc 5, dec 1*, rep 6 times. (36 sts)

R20: *Sc 4, dec 1*, rep 6 times. (30 sts)

R21–22: Sc 30.

Work on face: Attach eyes and embroider mouth. For cheeks, cut 2 circles from felt and sew to head.

R23: *Sc 3, dec 1*, rep 6 times. (24 sts)

R24: *Sc 2, dec 1*, rep 6 times. (18 sts)
Stuff body almost to top.

R25: *Sc 1, dec 1*, rep 6 times. (12 sts)
Finish stuffing.

R26: *Sk 1 sc, sc 1*, rep 6 times. (6 sts)
Fasten off and weave in ends.

ARMS (Make 8)

R1: Ch 2, 4 sc in second chain from hook.

R2: 2 sc in each sc around. (8 sts)

R3–11: Sc 8, stuffing as you go.

Fasten off, leaving a long tail for sewing. After all eight arms are finished, sew them evenly around the body.

BABY

HEAD AND BODY

R1: Ch 2, 6 sc in second chain from hook.

R2: 2 sc in each sc around. (12 sts)

R3: *Sc 1, 2 sc in next sc*, rep 6 times. (18 sts)

R4: *Sc 2, 2 sc in next sc*, rep 6 times. (24 sts)

R5: *Sc 3, 2 sc in next sc*, rep 6 times. (30 sts)

R6–11: Sc 30.

R12: *Sc 3, dec 1*, rep 6 times. (24 sts)

R13–15: Sc 24.

Work on face: Attach eyes and embroider mouth. For cheeks, cut 2 circles from felt and sew to head.

R16: *Sc 2, dec 1*, rep 6 times. (18 sts)
Stuff body almost to top.

R17: *Sc 1, dec 1*, rep 6 times. (12 sts)
Finish stuffing.

R18: *Sk 1 sc, sc 1*, rep 6 times. (6 sts)
Fasten off and weave in ends.

ARMS (Make 8)

R1: Ch 2, 3 sc in second chain from hook.

R2: 2 sc in each sc around (6 sts)

R3–6: Sc 6, stuffing as you go.

Fasten off, leaving a long tail for sewing. After all eight arms are finished, sew them evenly around the body.

Octopus cheek

These are the best plants for people who—just like me— can't take care of a real plant or who have an office without a window. Give them as computer friends to whoever will love them. It might also be the only time you get to cuddle with a cactus.

FINISHED SIZES

Mr. Cactus: Approx 6½"/16.5 cm tall
Mrs. Cactus: Approx 4½"/11.5 cm tall
Depending on your tension and yarn choice, finished sizes may vary.

MATERIALS

Worsted-weight yarn in green, orange, tan, and brown
Size G/6 (4.25 mm) crochet hook
9 mm plastic eyes with safety backings
Black embroidery floss and tapestry needle
Fiberfill or stuffing of your choice

MR. CACTUS

CACTUS

Using green yarn,

R1: Ch 2, 6 sc in second ch from hook.

R2: 2 sc in each sc around. (12 sts)

R3: *Sc 1, 2 sc in next sc*, rep 6 times. (18 sts)

R4: *Sc 2, 2 sc in next sc*, rep 6 times. (24 sts)

R5: *Sc 3, 2 sc in next sc*, rep 6 times. (30 sts)

R6: *Sc 4, 2 sc in next sc*, rep 6 times. (36 sts)

R7–26: Sc 36.

Work on face: Attach eyes and embroider mouth.

R27: *Sc 4, dec 1*, rep 6 times. (30 sts)

R28–31: Sc 30.

Change to tan yarn.

R32: Sc 30 through front loops only.

R33: *Sc 1, 2 sc in next sc*, rep 15 times. (45 sts)

R34: *Sc 2, 2 sc in next sc*, rep 15 times. (60 sts)

R35–37: Sc 60.

Fasten off, leaving a long tail for sewing, and set aside.

POT

Using brown yarn,

R1: Ch 2, 6 sc in second ch from hook.

R2: 2 sc in each sc around. (12 sts)

R3: *Sc 1, 2 sc in next sc*, rep 6 times. (18 sts)

R4: *Sc 2, 2 sc in next sc*, rep 6 times. (24 sts)

R5: *Sc 3, 2 sc in next sc*, rep 6 times. (30 sts)

R6: *Sc 4, 2 sc in next sc*, rep 6 times. (36 sts)

R7: *Sc 5, 2 sc in next sc*, rep 6 times. (42 sts)

R8: *Sc 6, 2 sc in next sc*, rep 6 times. (48 sts)

R9: *Sc 7, 2 sc in next sc*, rep 6 times. (54 sts)

R10: Sc 54.

R11: Through back loops only, *sc 7, dec 1*, rep 6 times. (48 sts)

R12: *Sc 7, 2 sc in next sc*, rep 6 times. (54 sts)

R13: *Sc 8, 2 sc in next sc*, rep 6 times. (60 sts)

R14–20: Sc 60.

Fasten off and weave in ends. Stuff cactus and pot and sew cactus to inside of pot approx ¼"/1 cm below rim.

MRS. CacTUS

FLOWER

Using white yarn,

R1: Ch 2, 10 sc in second ch from hook.

R2: 2 sc in each sc around. (20 sts)

R3: 2 sc in each sc around. (40 sts)

R4: 2 sc in each sc around. (80 sts)

R5: 2 sc in each sc around. (160 sts)

Fasten off and weave in ends.

CACTUS

Using orange yarn,

R1: Ch 2, 6 sc in second ch from hook.

R2: 2 sc in each sc around. (12 sts)

R3: *Sc 1, 2 sc in next sc*, rep 6 times. (18 sts)

R4: *Sc 2, 2 sc in next sc*, rep 6 times. (24 sts)

R5: *Sc 3, 2 sc in next sc*, rep 6 times. (30 sts)

R6: *Sc 4, 2 sc in next sc*, rep 6 times. (36 sts)

R7: *Sc 5, 2 sc in next sc*, rep 6 times. (42 sts)

R8: *Sc 6, 2 sc in next sc*, rep 6 times. (48 sts)

R9: *Sc 7, 2 sc in next sc*, rep 6 times. (54 sts)

R10: *Sc 8, 2 sc in next sc*, rep 6 times. (60 sts)

R11–20: Sc 60.

R21: *Sc 8, dec 1*, rep 6 times. (54 sts)

R22: *Sc 7, dec 1*, rep 6 times. (48 sts)

R23: *Sc 6, dec 1*, rep 6 times. (42 sts)

Change to tan yarn.

R24: Sc 42 through front loops only.

R25: *Sc 2, 2 sc in next sc*, rep 14 times. (56 sts)

R26: *Sc 3, 2 sc in next sc*, rep 14 times. (70 sts)

R27 and 28: Sc 70.

Fasten off, leaving a long tail for sewing, and set aside.

Work on face: Attach eyes and embroider mouth.

Sew flower in place with white yarn.

POT

Using brown yarn,

R1: Ch 2, 7 sc in second ch from hook.

R2: 2 sc in each sc around. (14 sts)

R3: *Sc 1, 2 sc in next sc*, rep 7 times. (21 sts)

R4: *Sc 2, 2 sc in next sc*, rep 7 times. (28 sts)

R5: *Sc 3, 2 sc in next sc*, rep 7 times. (35 sts)

R6: *Sc 4, 2 sc in next sc*, rep 7 times. (42 sts)

R7: *Sc 5, 2 sc in next sc*, rep 7 times. (49 sts)

R8: Sc 49.

R9: Through back loops only, *sc 5, dec 1*, rep 7 times. (42 sts)

R10: *Sc 5, 2 sc in next sc*, rep 7 times. (49 sts)

R11: *Sc 6, 2 sc in next sc*, rep 7 times. (56 sts)

R12: *Sc 7, 2 sc in next sc*, rep 7 times. (63 sts)

R13: *Sc 8, 2 sc in next sc*, rep 7 times. (70 sts)

R14–20: Sc 70.

Fasten off and weave in ends. Stuff cactus and pot, and sew cactus to inside of pot approx ¼"/1 cm below rim.

EGGZACTLY!

These eggs are a definite favorite among kids and grown-ups! I made them when I was on maternity leave and was going through a breakfast obsession. I usually don't eat breakfast, but back then we were going through eggs like we owned shares in a chicken farm! My daughter Oli and her friends love to see what's inside the eggs and they spend a lot of time taking them out of the egg crate and reorganizing them.

FINISHED SIZES

Whole egg: Approx 2½"/6.25 cm tall
Eggshell bottom: Approx 1½"/3.75 cm tall
Eggshell top: Approx 1¼"/3 cm tall
Chick: Approx 1¾"/4.5 cm tall
Depending on your tension and yarn choice, finished sizes may vary.

MATERIALS

Worsted-weight yarn in white, gold, and orange
Size F/4 5 (3.75 mm) and E/4 (3.5 mm) crochet hooks
6 mm plastic eyes with safety backings
Small pieces of tan craft felt
Sewing thread and sharp needle
Black embroidery floss and tapestry needle
Fiberfill or stuffing of your choice

WHOLE EGG

Using F hook and white yarn,

R1: Ch 2, 5 sc in second ch from hook.

R2: 2 sc in each sc around. (10 sts)

R3: *Sc 1, 2 sc in next sc*, rep 5 times. (15 sts)

R4: Sc 15.

R5: *Sc 2, 2 sc in next sc*, rep 5 times. (20 sts)

R6: *Sc 3, 2 sc in next sc*, rep 5 times. (25 sts)

R7–13: Sc 25.

R14: *Sc 3, dec 1*, rep 5 times. (20 sts)

Work on face: Attach eyes and embroider mouth. For cheeks, cut 2 circles from felt and sew in place.

R15: *Sc 2, dec 1*, rep 5 times. (15 sts)

R16: Sc 15.

Stuff.

R17: *Sc 1, dec 1*, rep 5 times. (10 sts)

R18: *Sk 1 sc, sc 1*, rep 5 times. (5 sts)

Fasten off and weave in ends.

EGGSHELL

EGGSHELL BOTTOM

Using F hook and white yarn,

R1: Ch 2, 5 sc in second ch from hook.

R2: 2 sc in each sc around. (10 sts)

R3: *Sc 1, 2 sc in next sc*, rep 5 times. (15 sts)

R4: Sc 15.

R5: *Sc 2, 2 sc in next sc*, rep 5 times. (20 sts)

R6: *Sc 3, 2 sc in next sc*, rep 5 times. (25 sts)

R7–9: Sc 25.

R10: BPsc 25.

R11: *Sc 3, dec 1*, rep 5 times. (20 sts)

R12: Sc 20, sl st in next sc.

Fasten off and weave in ends.

EGGSHELL TOP

Using F hook and white yarn,

R1: Ch 2, 5 sc in second ch from hook.

R2: 2 sc in each sc around. (10 sts)

R3: *Sc 1, 2 sc in next sc*, rep 5 times. (15 sts)

R4: Sc 15.

R5: *Sc 2, 2 sc in next sc*, rep 5 times. (20 sts)

R6: *Sc 3, 2 sc in next sc*, rep 5 times. (25 sts)

R7–10: Sc 25.

Fasten off and weave in ends.

CHICK

Using E hook and gold or orange yarn,

R1: Ch 2, 5 sc in second ch from hook.

R2: 2 sc in each sc around. (10 sts)

R3: *Sc 1, 2 sc in next sc*, rep 5 times. (15 sts)

R4: *Sc 2, 2 sc in next sc*, rep 5 times. (20 sts)

R5–10: Sc 20.

Work on face: Attach eyes. Cut beak from felt and sew in place.

R11: *Sc 2, dec 1*, rep 5 times. (15 sts)

R12: Sc 15.

Stuff almost to top.

R13: *Sc 1, dec 1*, rep 5 times. (10 sts)

Finish stuffing.

R14: *Sk 1 sc, sc 1*, rep 5 times. (5 sts)

Fasten off and weave in ends.

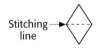

Stitching line

Chick beak

Egg cheek

What can be better than a smiling dessert? I bet you they're smiling because you can make as many cupcakes and ice-cream cones and café con leche cups as you want and never, ever grow tired of looking at them . . . and they know it. (They make great pincushions, too!)

FINISHED SIZES

Café con Leche cup: Approx 1¾"/4.5 cm tall
Cupcake: Approx 2"/5 cm tall
Ice-cream cone: Approx 3¼"/8.25 cm tall
Depending on your tension and yarn choice, finished sizes may vary.

MATERIALS

Worsted-weight yarn in blue, tan, bright pink, light pink, and brown
Size F/5 (4mm) crochet hook
6 mm plastic eyes with safety backings
Small piece of pink craft felt
Sewing thread and sharp needle
Black embroidery floss and tapestry needle
Small seed beads in assorted colors for cupcake
Fiberfill or stuffing of your choice

Café con Leche Cup

CUP

Using blue yarn,

R1: Ch 2, 7 sc in second ch from hook.

R2: 2 sc in each sc around. (14 sts)

R3: *Sc 1, 2 sc in next sc*, rep 7 times. (21 sts)

R4: *Sc 2, 2 sc in next sc*, rep 7 times. (28 sts)

R5: *Sc 3, 2 sc in next sc*, rep 7 times. (35 sts)

R6: Through back loops only, *sc 3, dec 1*, rep 7 times. (28 sts)

R7–15: Sc 28.

Fasten off and weave in ends.

Work on face: Attach eyes and embroider mouth. For cheeks, cut 2 circles of pink felt and sew in place.

HANDLE

Using blue yarn,

Ch 14, hdc 12 starting in third ch from hook.

Fasten off, leaving long tail for sewing. Weave in ends and sew to mug.

CAFÉ CON LECHE

Using tan yarn,

R1: Ch 2, 5 sc in second ch from hook.

R2: 2 sc in each sc around. (10 sts)

R3: *Sc 1, 2 sc in next sc*, rep 5 times. (15 sts)

R4: *Sc 2, 2 sc in next sc*, rep 5 times. (20 sts)

R5: *Sc 3, 2 sc in next sc*, rep 5 times. (25 sts)

Stuff mug and sew café con leche to inside of mug, about ½"/1 cm below rim.

Cup cheek

Cupcake

BOTTOM

Using tan yarn,

R1: Ch 2, 6 sc in second ch from hook.

R2: 2 sc in each sc around. (12 sts)

R3: *1 sc, 2 sc in next sc*, rep 6 times. (18 sts)

R4: *2 sc, 2 sc in next sc*, rep 6 times. (24 sts)

R5: *3 sc, 2 sc in next sc*, rep 6 times. (30 sts)

R6: Through back loops only, *sc 3, dec 1*, rep 6 times. (24 sts)

R7: *3 sc, 2 sc in next sc*, rep 6 times. (30 sts)

R8–11: Sc 30.

Fasten off, leaving a long tail for sewing, and set aside.

Work on face: Attach eyes and embroider mouth.

ICING

Using light pink yarn,

R1: Ch 2, 6 sc in second ch from hook.

R2: 2 sc in each sc around. (12 sts)

R3: *1 sc, 2 sc in next sc*, rep 6 times. (18 sts)

R4: *2 sc, 2 sc in next sc*, rep 6 times. (24 sts)

R5: *3 sc, 2 sc in next sc*, rep 6 times. (30 sts)

R6–9: Sc 30.

R10: *4 sc in next sc, sk 1 sc, sl st 1*, rep 10 times.

Fasten off and weave in ends. Using a sharp needle and sewing thread, sew seed bead "sprinkles" to icing.

FINISHING

Place the icing on top of the cupcake, lining up the stitches of the bottom with the stitches inside the wavy part of the top (don't sew into the wavy portion). Sew three-quarters of the way around and stuff the bottom with fiberfill so the cupcake sits nice and flat. Stuff the cupcake and icing with fiberfill. Finish sewing all the way around.

ice-Cream Cone

CONE

Using tan yarn,

R1: Ch 2, sc 4 in second ch from hook.

R2: Sc 4.

R3: *Sc 1, 2 sc in next sc*, rep twice. (6 sts)

R4: Sc 6.

R5: *Sc 1, 2 sc in next sc*, rep 3 times. (9 sts)

R6: Sc 9.

R7: *Sc 2, 2 sc in next sc*, rep 3 times. (12 sts)

R8: *Sc 1, 2 sc in next sc*, rep 6 times. (18 sts)

R9–11: Sc 18, sl st to first st of rnd.

Fasten off, leaving a long tail for sewing, and set aside.

ICE CREAM

Using bright pink yarn,

R1: Ch 2, 6 sc in second ch from hook.

R2: 2 sc in each sc around. (12 sts)

R3: *1 sc, 2 sc in next sc*, rep 6 times. (18 sts)

R4: *2 sc, 2 sc in next sc*, rep 6 times. (24 sts)

R5: *3 sc, 2 sc in next sc*, rep 6 times. (30 sts)

R6–12: Sc 30.

R13: *Sc 3, dec 1*, rep 6 times. (24 sts)

Work on face: Attach eyes and embroider mouth.

R14: *Sc 2, dec 1*, rep 6 times. (18 sts)

Stuff almost full.

R15: *Sc 1, dec 1*, rep 6 times. (12 sts)

Finish stuffing, fasten off, and weave in ends. Stuff cone and sew to ice cream.

CHOCOLATE TOPPING

Using brown yarn,

R1: Ch 2, 6 sc in second ch from hook.

R2: 2 sc in each sc around. (12 sts)

R3: *1 sc, 2 sc in next sc*, rep 6 times. (18 sts)

R4: *2 sc, 2 sc in next sc*, rep 6 times. (24 sts)

R5: Sc 24.

R6: *3 hdc in next sc, sk 1 sc, sl st in next sc*, rep 8 times.

Fasten off, leaving a long tail for sewing, and sew to top of ice cream.

aMi
STaCK-
UP

The basic instructions are the same for each of the seven tiny amis pictured. The ears vary, as do the feet for the duck and the shell for the itty-bitty turtle. So choose your yarn colors and crochet the body, head, and legs following the basic directions. Choose the type of ears you need and refer to the photo for the facial details you'd like your little critter to have. It's just that easy.

FiNiSHCD SiZeS

Each animal: Approx 3"/7.5 cm tall
Depending on your tension and yarn choice, finished sizes may vary.

MaTeRiaLS

Worsted-weight yarn in assorted colors
Size F/5 (4 mm) and E/4 (3.50 mm) crochet hooks
6 mm plastic eyes with safety backings
Small pieces of craft felt for faces
Sewing thread and sharp needle
Black, pink, and brown embroidery floss and tapestry needle
Fiberfill or stuffing of your choice

Bear front

Bear back

Turtle front

Tiny Ami

HEAD

Using F hook,

R1: Ch 2, 6 sc in second ch from hook.

R2: 2 sc in each sc around. (12 sts)

R3: *Sc 1, 2 sc in next sc*, rep 6 times. (18 sts)

R4: *Sc 2, 2 sc in next sc*, rep 6 times. (24 sts)

R5–11: Sc 24.

R12: *Sc 2, dec 1*, rep 6 times. (18 sts)

Work on faces: For all animals, attach eyes. For bear, cut eye circles from felt, make a small slit in the circles, and insert eyes. For bear, cat, bunny, mouse, and monkey, cut muzzle from felt, embroider nose and mouth, and sew muzzle to head. For turtle, embroider nose and mouth. For cat, embroider whiskers to face after

sewing on muzzle.

R13: *Sc 1, dec 1*, rep 6 times. (12 sts)

Stuff head.

R14: *Sk 1 sc, sc 1*, rep 6 times. (6 sts)

Fasten off, and weave in loose ends.

BODY

Using F hook,

R1: Ch 2, 5 sc in second ch from hook.

R2: 2 sc in each sc around. (10 sts)

R3: *1 sc, 2 sc in next sc*, rep 5 times. (15 sts)

R4–7:** Sc 15.

****If you're planning to give your toy a skirt, crochet R5 through back loops only (you'll use the front loops later when making the skirt). R6 and R7 are crocheted the usual way.

Turtle side

R8: *Sc 1, dec 1*, rep 5 times. (10 sts)

Fasten off, leaving a long tail for sewing. Stuff and sew body to head.

Mouse front

Duck front

Duck side

Mouse back

(Make 2 of each for each animal)

These are the same for all the animals except the duck (see page 72).

Using E hook,

R1: Ch 2, 3 sc in second ch from hook.

R2: 2 sc in each sc around. (6 sts)

R3 and 4: Sc 6.

Fasten off, leaving a long tail for sewing. Sew open end tog and sew to body (no need to stuff legs and arms). Note that if you're making the turtle, you should sew on shell (see page 72) before sewing on arms and legs.

SKIRT FOR MOUSE

Using F hook,

Holding toy upside down (head down), join yarn at back to one of front loops you left when making body.

R1: Sc 15.

R2: *Sc 2, 2 sc in next sc*, rep 5 times. (20 sts)

R3: Sc 20.

Fasten off and weave in loose ends.

SCARF FOR BEAR

Using E hook,

Loosely ch 40, turn.

Ch 1, sc in second ch from hook and in each ch across.

Fasten off and weave in ends.

HAT FOR BUNNY

Using F hook,

R1: Ch 2, 7 sc in second ch from hook.

R2: 2 sc in each sc around. (14 sts)

R3: *Sc 1, 2 sc in next sc*, rep 7 times. (21 sts)

R4: *Sc 2, 2 sc in next sc*, rep 7 times. (28 sts)

R5–9: Sc 28.

Fasten off and weave in ends.

EaRS AND OTHER DeTaiLS

Follow the directions for the particular animal you're making.

BEAR AND MONKEY EARS (Make 2)

Using E hook,

R1: Ch 2, 4 sc in second ch from hook.

R2: 2 sc in each sc around. (8 sts)

R3: Sc 8. Join with sl st.

Fasten off, leaving a long tail for sewing. Sew open end tog and sew to head.

BUNNY EARS (Make 2)

Using E hook,

R1: Ch 14, turn.

R2: Hdc in third ch from hook and in next 10 sts. 5 hdc in next st (you should now be on the other side of the ch), hdc 12.

Fasten off, leaving a long tail for sewing. Cut inner ear from felt, whipstitch to inside of crocheted ear, and sew ear to head.

TURTLE SHELL

Using F hook,

R1: Ch 2, 5 sc in second ch from hook.

R2: 2 Sc in each sc around. (10 sts)

R3: *Sc 1, 2 sc in next sc*, rep 5 times. (15 sts)

R4–6: Sc 15.

R7: *Sc 2, 2 sc in next sc*, rep 5 times. (20 sts)

R8: Sc 20.

Fasten off, leaving a long tail for sewing. Sew to back, approx three-quarters of the way around, stuff, and finish sewing.

MOUSE EARS (Make 2)

Using E hook,

Ch 2, 7 sc in second ch from hook.

Fasten off, leaving a long tail for sewing, and sew to head.

CAT EARS (Make 2)

Using E hook,

R1: Ch 2, sc 5 in second ch from hook.

R2: Sc 5.

R3: Sc 2 in each sc around. (10 sts)

Fasten off, leaving a long tail for sewing. Sew open end tog and sew to head.

CAT TAIL

Using E hook,

Make a chain the desired tail length and sew to cat's body.

DUCK BEAK, LEGS, AND WINGS

There's no need to stuff any of these pieces.

Using E hook,

R1: Ch 2, 4 sc in second ch from hook.

R2: 2 sc in each sc around. (8 sts)

For beak:

R3: Sc 8.

Bunny front

Bunny back

Fasten off, leaving a long tail for sewing. Sew open end tog and sew to head.

For legs and wings (make 2 of each):

R3–4: Sc 8.

Fasten off, leaving a long tail for sewing. Sew open end tog and sew to body.

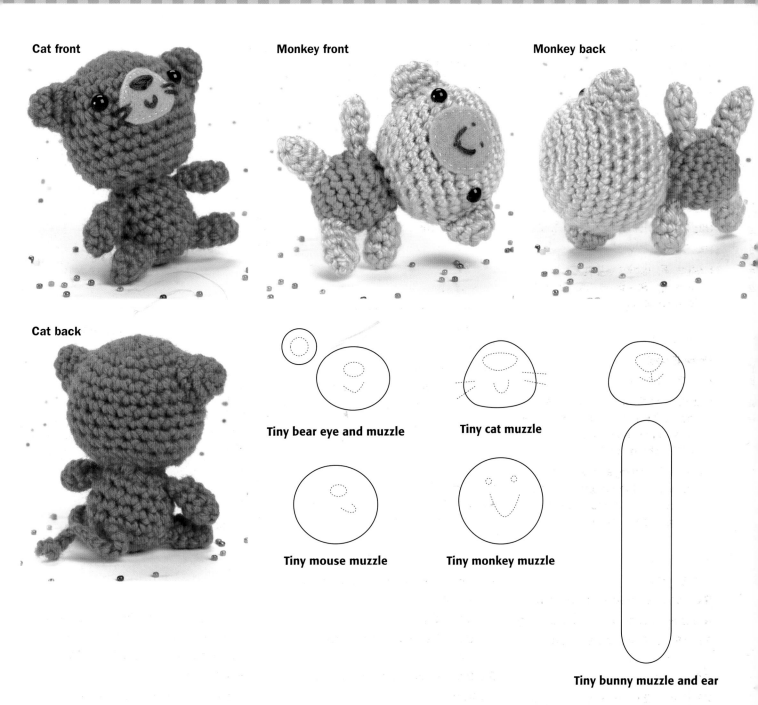

Cat front

Monkey front

Monkey back

Cat back

Tiny bear eye and muzzle

Tiny cat muzzle

Tiny mouse muzzle

Tiny monkey muzzle

Tiny bunny muzzle and ear

How many times can a kid hear "eat your fruit"?
Maybe we should start saying "hug your fruit."
Who knows, befriending a pear might be the
beginning of a wonderful, fruity friendship.

FiNiSHeD SiZe

Approx 3"/7.5 cm tall
Depending on your tension and yarn choice, finished sizes may vary.

MaTeRiaLS

Worsted-weight yarn in green and brown
Size F/5 (4mm) crochet hook
9 mm plastic eyes with safety backings
Small pieces of pink craft felt
Sewing thread and sharp needle
Black embroidery floss and tapestry needle
Fiberfill or stuffing of your choice

Pear

Pear is worked from the bottom up (keep that in mind when working on the face).

With green yarn,

R1: Ch 2, 6 sc in second ch from hook.

R2: 2 sc in each sc around. (12 sts)

R3: *Sc 1, 2 sc in next sc*, rep 6 times. (18 sts)

R4: *Sc 2, 2 sc in next sc*, rep 6 times. (24 sts)

R5: *Sc 3, 2 sc in next sc*, rep 6 times. (30 sts)

R6: *Sc 4, 2 sc in next sc*, rep 6 times. (36 sts)

R7: *Sc 5, 2 sc in next sc*, rep 6 times. (42 sts)

R8–16: Sc 42.

R17: *Sc 5, dec 1*, rep 6 times. (36 sts)

R18: *Sc 4, dec 1*, rep 6 times. (30 sts)

R19 and 20: Sc 30.

Work on face: Attach eyes and embroider mouth. For cheeks, cut 2 circles from pink felt and sew in place.

R21: *Sc 3, dec 1*, rep 6 times. (24 sts)

R22–24: Sc 24.

R25: *Sc 2, dec 1*, rep 6 times. (18 sts)

Stuff almost to top.

R26: *Sc 1, dec 1*, rep 6 times. (12 sts)

Finish stuffing.

R27: *Sk 1 sc, sc 1*, rep 6 times. (6 sts)

Fasten off and weave in ends.

STEM

Using brown yarn,

Ch 5, sc 4 starting at second ch from hook.

Fasten off, leaving a long tail for sewing, and sew to pear.

LEAF

Using brown yarn,

Ch 8, and starting at second bump (the bumps are on opposite side, or behind the braidlike ch where you usually crochet) from hook:

Sl st 1, sc 1, dc 1, tr 1, dc 1, sc 1, sl st 1, rep once on opposite side (which now looks like regular sc because you crocheted in the bumps).

Fasten off, leaving a long tail for sewing, and sew to pear.

Pear cheek

An apple a day . . . should put a smile on your face,
especially when it's hanging out with such an odd friend!
This pair would make a great present for
your favorite teacher or apple lover.

FINISHED SIZE

Approx 3" wide x 2" tall/7.5 cm x 5 cc
Depending on your tension and yarn choice, finished sizes may vary.

MATERIALS

Worsted-weight yarn in red, green, and brown
Size F/5 (4mm) crochet hook
9 and 6 mm plastic eyes with safety backings
Black embroidery floss and tapestry needle
Fiberfill or stuffing of your choice

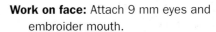

LiTTLe aPPLe WiTH WORM

STEM

Using brown yarn,

Ch 5, sc 4 starting at second ch from hook.

Fasten off, leaving a long tail for sewing, and set aside.

LEAF

Using green yarn,

Ch 8, and starting at second bump (the "bumps" are on the opposite side of, or behind, the braidlike ch where you usually crochet) from hook,

Sl st 1, sc 1, dc 1, tr 1, dc 1, sc 1, sl st 1, rep on the opposite side (which now looks like regular sc because you crocheted in the bumps)

Fasten off, leaving a long tail for sewing, and set aside.

APPLE

Using red yarn,

R1: Ch 2, 6 sc in second ch from hook.

R2: 2 sc in each sc around. (12 sts)

R3: *Sc 1, 2 sc in next sc*, rep 6 times. (18 sts)

R4: *Sc 2, 2 sc in next sc*, rep 6 times. (24 sts)

R5: *Sc 3, 2 sc in next sc*, rep 6 times. (30 sts)

R6: *Sc 4, 2 sc in next sc*, rep 6 times. (36 sts)

R7: *Sc 5, 2 sc in next sc*, rep 6 times. (42 sts)

R8–17: Sc 42.

R18: *Sc 5, dec 1*, rep 6 times. (36 sts)

R19: *Sc 4, dec 1*, rep 6 times. (30 sts)

R20: *Sc 3, dec 1*, rep 6 times. (24 sts)

Work on face: Attach 9 mm eyes and embroider mouth.

Sew stem and leaf to top of apple (it's easier to attach them now when you can work from the inside).

R21: *Sc 2, dec 1*, rep 6 times. (18 sts)

R22: Sc 18.

Stuff almost to the top.

R23: *Sc 1, dec 1*, rep 6 times. (12 sts)

Finish stuffing.

R24: *Sk 1 sc, sc 1*, rep 6 times. (6 sts)

Fasten off, and weave in ends.

WORM

Using green yarn,

R1: Ch 2, 8 sc in second ch from hook.

R2–4: Sc 8.

Work on face: Attach 6 mm eyes and embroider mouth.

R5 and 6: Sc 8, stuffing as you go.

R7: Sc 4 through back loops only, sc 4.

R8: Hdc 4, sc 4.

R9: Sc 4.

Fasten off, leaving a long tail for sewing, and sew to apple.

YARN

Patons
www.patonsyarns.com

Caron
www.caron.com

Red Heart
www.coatsandclark.com

Bernat
www.bernat.com

SAFETY EYES

Your local craft store probably carries safety eyes. If you can't find them locally, try visiting www.sunshinecrafts.com; search for "eyes." They ship them fast.

MUSHROOM DECORATIONS ON HEDGEHOGS

www.smallstump.com

aBOUT THe aUTHOR

Ana Paula Rímoli was born in Montevideo, Uruguay, where she was always making stuff. She started crocheting when she was little, sitting outside one summer afternoon with her neighbor lending instruction. She started with scarves and granny squares and little bags and never stopped. When her oldest daughter was born, she started crocheting little toys for her and later discovered amigurumi. Ana's been "hooked" ever since, and the toy collection is growing and growing, slowly taking over the whole house!

Ana now lives in New Jersey with her two little girls and never-ending source of inspiration, Oli and Martina, and her super-nice husband who supports her yarn obsession.